AF270170

What people are saying about
MOVE OR DIE

"Chris helped set the foundation for the Super Bowl Champion in Seattle with his innovative approach to developing and nurturing elite athletes…integral to the most successful programs in the history of the sport."

—Bruce Feldman,
ESPN, FOX Sports Writer,
Analyst, *New York Times* Best Selling Author

"(Chris') lessons, words, visions, and inspirational stories not only impacted me in the NFL, but as a man. I am grateful for his significance in my life from the moment I met him. We either 'move' or we 'die.'"

—Russell Wilson,
NFL Quarterback

"*Move or Die* is a must read for anyone navigating today's leadership challenges. Chris's guidance comes from the heart with life learnings from the playing field one can take to the corporate world."

—Rosemary St.Clair,
Veteran NIKE Executive,
Vice President & General Manager,
Nike Global Women (retired)

"Winston Churchill said that he spent ninety percent of his time coming up with good answers to tough questions. *Move or Die* dives into precisely that. This generous gift of guidance is about your life and how every move is a game changer."

—Scott L. Christensen,
Artist

Move or Die

Creating a Game Plan from Stuck to Significance

CHRIS CARLISLE

Made for Success Publishing
P.O. Box 1775 Issaquah, WA 98027
www.MadeForSuccessPublishing.com

Distributed by Made for Success Publishing

First Printing

Library of Congress Cataloging-in-Publication data
    Carlisle, Chris
    MOVE OR DIE: Creating a Game-Plan from Stuck to Significance
    p. cm.
    LCCN: 2021952509
    ISBN: 979-8-21202-865-2 (*Paperback*)
    ISBN: 978-1-64146-743-8 (*eBook*)
    ISBN: 978-1-64146-666-0 (*Audiobook*)

Printed in the United States of America

For further information contact Made for Success Publishing
+14255266480 or email service@madeforsuccess.net

Acknowledgements

So, I finally wrote that book I had been working on for what seemed like forever. Every word I typed brought back memories of all of the people who helped develop my Move or Die philosophy.

Hearing the echo of distant voices made me laugh and cry in the same measure as I wrote this book. The hardest thing was when it came time to edit the 600-pages. Unfortunately, the part I wrote about you was surgically removed by the world's greatest editor, Katie Rios. But, not to worry, she said your name and story would be in my next book.

I also would like to thank my publishing team, led by Bryan and DeeDee Heathman. They took my notebooks, full of stories and stick-figure drawings, and rendered them down into this book. I couldn't have done this without y'all!

I want to thank all the people that have meant so much in my life. All the teachers, students, athletes, and people I have worked with. Each of you has left your mark in my life, and I can only hope that I helped you move closer towards your ultimate goals.

To Mom and Dad, Ed Lenius, Father William Wewers and the entire monastic community at Subiaco Abbey, Dr. George Morgan, Cleo & Frances Pope, Delores & Don Sims, Noreen Coyan, Tim & Bobbi Weiss, and my family, you have taught me that success is what you do for yourself. Still, significance is what you do to help others succeed.

To my "Quarters," Keith Sims, Todd Pierce, Scott Christensen, Rod & Jacque Coyan, and Bobby & Jill Sewell, thank you for always having the strength and conviction to tell me THE truth. Because of your love and friendship, I have moved down my path with great confidence.

Finally, to my wife Louon and my son Alex, I know it hasn't been easy traveling around the country doing this coaching thing, but we have always laughed and loved! Thanks for putting up with me!

One last story: We went into my son's first-grade class for a parent-teacher meeting. The teacher had high praise for Alex as far as his academics went. His only glitch was, "He always has to be first. First in line for recess, first in line for lunch, first in line for reading, first in line for everything." Louon looked at me, holding back a laugh, as I looked quizzically at the teacher and asked, "So what is the problem …?"

We have two choices … Move or Die … you decide!!!

Contents

FOREWORD 13

INTRODUCTION: THE PATH TO SIGNIFICANCE ... 15

CHAPTER 1: HARD LESSONS 21

Sticking Point #1: Arrogance 23

Sticking Point #2: Ignorance 26

Learning to Learn 31

Sticking Point #3: Inflexibility 32

Be the Best 37

CHAPTER 2: WHICH ONE ARE YOU? 39

Know Your *Who* 43

Preparation 46

Build a Bridge 47

Find a New Way 49

Know Your *What* 50

Not Using All Your Crayons 55

Know Your *Why* 59

No Excuses 61

CHAPTER 3: THE DEEP END 65

Doubting Our Destiny 70
Key #1: Understand Yourself 71
Key #2: Surround Yourself with People You Trust 73
We Few, We Happy Few 76
Key #3: Cultivating Trust 79
Communication: Earning Trust 80
Consistency: Routine and Expectations 81
Caring: Employee / Employer.. 82
It All Comes Down to Trust.. 85

CHAPTER 4: SPEAK YOUR TRUTH 87

Use Your Gifts! 90
A King Ain't Satisfied 92
Putting Dreams into Action.. 95
Lead by Example 97
Are You Willing? 98

CHAPTER 5: GRIND 101

Step One: Passion 104
Step Two: Prepare 105
Step Three: Practice 106
Step Four: Perform 107
Step Five: Perseverance 108
Pursuing the Horizon 109
Don't Quit 111
Now, Get to Work! 113

CHAPTER 6: TAKE THE RISK 115

The Good, the Bad and the Ugly.. 117
Risk Assessment System: Going Through My Choices 123
Perspective is Everything.. 126
Is This Really It? 127
My Next Move.. 129

CHAPTER 7: THE ROAD LESS TRAVELED 133

    Recognize: Understand There is a Problem.............. 136

    Research: Find Answers to the Problems.............. 137

    Receptive: Find Fertile Ground 138

    Reach: Grow the Seed.................. 139

    React: The Evolution of New Ideas 139

    My Five Rs 141

    Taking Flight.................. 143

    Outside the Music Box 144

    Trendsetters.................. 145

    Doing Things Better 146

CHAPTER 8: LEAVE YOUR MARK.................. 149

    A Legacy of Leaving a Mark.................. 150

    Gifts: How to Leave Your Mark 152

    Grinders (Hard Workers) 153

    Internally Driven (Highly Motivated)................. 154

    Focused (Goal-Oriented) 154

    Transformative (They Change and Affect Change)......... 155

    Synergetic (Path Makers) 156

    Success vs. Significance 157

    Two Paths Converge.................. 157

    Not Just a Comic Strip 159

    More Than a Football Star 160

    Is it Repeatable? 162

    My Mark 164

    It's Your Turn 165

CONCLUSION: KEEP MOVING
DOWN THE LINE!.................. 167

THE GAME PLAN 169

    Chapter 1: Hard Lessons 171

    Chapter 2: Which One Are You?................. 173

Chapter 3: The Deep End 174

Chapter 4: Speak Your Truth 176

Chapter 5: Grind 177

Chapter 6: Take the Risk 179

Chapter 7: The Road Less Traveled 180

Chapter 8: Leave Your Mark.................................... 181

Onward 183

ABOUT THE AUTHOR...................................... 185

Foreword

I first became aware of Chris Carlisle after I was named the head football coach of the University of Southern California. I called my good friend, John Stucky, who was running the strength program at the University of Tennessee at the time, and asked him who was the best coach on his staff. I regarded John Stucky as the best strength and conditioning coach in college football, and I knew whoever he called his top guy was the second best. He gave me Chris's name and number, and I called him up. Chris told me he had been diagnosed with Hodgkin's disease, and my only question was, does that mean you can't coach as well? He emphatically replied with a "No sir," and I asked if he could be here on Monday.

For the next 18 years, we developed a friendship and program that would take two organizations to the top of the game, winning a Super Bowl, two college football national championships and seven consecutive PAC-10 championships. Chris played a big part in the preparation of the athletes, but the biggest role that he played was as a messaging agent for me.

When you are developing a culture, a head football coach is the main voice of the team. But it is essential that you have a person who, using their own voice, passes on the message daily. As a head coach, I wasn't able to be with the players too much. In the winter, it was because of recruiting, and in the summer, the NCAA rules stated that a football coach wasn't allowed to watch (or really even be around the players). This is a crucial 16 weeks (8 in the spring and 8 in the summer), and I needed a person who understood my vision and was a loyal lieutenant.

Coach C, as Coach Carlisle was known to all of our athletes, was the best at this. He made a difference with each athlete daily—not only physically but also in developing the "always compete" attitude that we needed to build a successful organization. His ability to motivate the least motivated was an everyday sort of thing. Where he excelled was continuing to motivate those who were at the top of their game. In sports, as it is in life, when people get to the top, they have a tendency to relax. Chris would not have that for a minute. All-Conference players one year would become All-Americans the next. All-Americans would then become Heisman Trophy winners and first-round draft choices.

One of the things I quickly learned about Coach C was that he had a wealth of knowledge in the area of history and a natural talent for storytelling. He could take three totally different entities and weave them into a teachable moment that not only the players would take away, but the entire football staff and anyone lucky enough to hear his Friday walkthrough masterclass on motivation!

The players couldn't wait for the story of the week when we traveled. I would look around the room, and the entire team would be held spell-bound as Chris recreated a story from history that corresponded with our location but also with the message I needed to have repeated each week.

This went so well in college that I had him do the same thing when we got to the Seattle Seahawks. It soon got to a point where Chris's ability to lift the team with his words became contagious with the rest of the staff. Meetings that could be boring were now must-see events. People from other departments would stand at the back to hear Chris do his "Hey Coach C, Where the F#@k Are We Going" presentation.

This book is like listening to my old friend tell stories, and I have no doubt he will make a difference in anyone's life that is willing to lean in, listen, and put in the work.

—Pete Caroll,
Championship Coach and Author

THE PATH TO SIGNIFICANCE

> The key to realizing a dream is to focus not on success but on significance—and then even the small steps and little victories along the path will take on greater meaning.
> — Oprah Winfrey

Move or die—they are the two choices we were all born with.

Anthropologists have found that we were born with a genetic need to *move* dating back to our earliest ancestors. This need to move was satisfied easily early in our history, but it is becoming more and more difficult as time goes on—mostly because we've become complacent, satisfied with our lives the way they are with no desire to change (not to mention the lack of time we spend outside!).

Now, the question is, how do we feed this genetic need?

Spoiler alert: It's not about exercising more. It's about constantly moving forward in *all* aspects of our lives. Whether it's personal, professional, physical, emotional, or social, we need to keep moving forward—keep moving down the line.

If we cease to move, we get stuck, we stagnate, and we die… and 50 years later, they bury us. Inside, we have ceased to be vital. We stop dreaming and just exist. We no longer work to accomplish our dreams, but we toil to make real the dreams of others.

A couple of years ago, I was doing research for a book I was writing on the importance of training movement in sports when I found a study on how movement is a genetic need in all humans. I sat back and reflected on how movement has been the basis of all success in human history, and on the flip side, that lack of movement is the core of defeat. I then looked at my own life and saw how I unknowingly followed that genetic need to move throughout my personal and professional life, clearing and creating a path to success and significance.

I began to see that the path I had walked from being a kid born with a physical handicap and speech impediment to becoming a Super Bowl-winning coach and a motivational speaker had a specific sequence of mile markers. I use the term "path" because I've observed that often we travel on a circuitous route from where we begin to where we want to be. Sometimes people end up at the destination they had hoped, but sadly, too many times they get sidetracked and fall short.

No matter how we get to where we end up or how long it takes us, we take steps to get to that end place. Along that path, we come to dead ends, brick walls, doors that need keys to open them, shortcuts, and divergences—all of which call for us to make decisions.

Every day, we are confronted with these decisions. "Should I do *this,* or should I do *that*?" Oftentimes, we throw caution to the wind and simply go with our best guess. Yet, with each decision we make, we must also face the consequence of our decision, whether good or bad, and keep walking down that path. If we find out that was the right move, we are emboldened. However, when we find that it was the wrong decision, we become timid in our decision-making moving forward—mostly out of fear of making a mistake. Time and time again, I have seen people become afraid and thus cease to continue moving forward along their path. Instead of fighting for their dreams, they stop, they get stuck, they stagnate, and their dreams die.

But that doesn't have to be the case. There's a better way. We can keep moving down the line toward our goals but we need a game plan that will get us there!

What if you had the opportunity to reduce the risk of your decisions? How valuable would that be to you?

This is precisely why I wrote the book you're holding in your hands. I have lived through six decades. I have been a student of life and a professional watcher of human nature. For 35 years, my career as a teacher and coach took me from small high schools in Nebraska and Arkansas to the biggest theaters of sport, NCAA championships, and the Super Bowl. The athletes, coaches, staff, and students who have passed through my "laboratory" have graciously shared their stories with me and had a hand in showing me how to do things right and how to do things wrong. It was as simple as taking time to observe the theatre of life played out in front of me every day for over 35 years.

Just think of the thousands of "test cases" I was able to observe. I took copious amounts of notes and kept index cards with the actions and following reactions of my students and athletes. The byproduct of these case studies was a pattern of behaviors which led people just like you to successfully maximize their potential and pave a path to significance.

A perfect example of an individual moving down the line from leading an average life to becoming successful and then ascending to significance occurred in the spring of 2011 when I had the great fortune to meet Doug Baldwin. Doug was a rookie free agent from Stanford who had joined the team I was with, the Seattle Seahawks. I liked him from the first moment I met him. He was a no-nonsense straight talker who didn't try to be anyone other than himself. He knew who he was and would walk through fire to obtain his dream.

Over the eight years that followed, I learned more and more about Doug. He was a student of life and the game of football. He was talented but not "gifted," athletically speaking. This just meant he needed to work harder than other players. His ability to grind and persevere was legendary, and his workouts broke many of those who tried to match him. He pushed himself relentlessly to become the best in the game—which he achieved. Doug went on to help his teammates win a Super Bowl and was named twice as a Pro Bowl player.

His greatest strengths, however, were not on the field or in the weight room. No, his greatest strengths were in his understanding of who he was. Believe it or not, this is one of the hardest things for a person to do—to understand who and what they are truly meant to be. Some people go through life having only listened to the expectations of other people, believing that those expectations were what they were destined to be. However, Doug knew what he was destined to be and do as a young boy, which gave him a burning desire to then accomplish his dreams; being an NFL football player and achieving it at any cost.

Some people called him "Angry Doug" because of his intensity. But the truth was, he was simply never satisfied with anything but the best. No one half-stepped it around Doug. Those who did would understand quickly that they had stepped into a world of hurt. Doug was able to call others out because he held himself to the same (high) standards every day. Because of this consistency both on and off the field, he earned the trust and respect of his teammates.

He could have stopped right there, having seen his dream of being in the NFL come to pass, but he didn't. Doug went on to earn his degree from Stanford, he was seen as one of the best players in the game, and he won a Super Bowl. Doug had maximized his potential to the nth degree; what else did he need to do?

But being successful was not what Doug lived his life for. No, he had bigger plans for his future. As he built his reputation on the football field, he also began to use his influence to reach out and build bridges. His work with police and community relations and his fight for criminal justice reform and educational change took him to a place of becoming *significant*. He not only used his talents to make his own life better, but he used his status to make the lives of others better and leave a mark on the world for all those who desire to follow in his footsteps to see.

This is just one person I was blessed to have watched grow and move forward as he carved out and followed a path to significance. Now, you may be thinking that I have a skewed reference group.

"Chris, you have star athletes and coaches as your reference material. What about the 'normal' people?"

Though it's true I've had the privilege to work with incredibly talented people; you would be surprised by just how "human" they actually are. In fact, they are gifted and flawed, simultaneously.

In the pages that follow, you will also learn about *my* path to significance. The route I took as a kid who was told time and time again that he wasn't good enough to live his dream life. You better believe I'll share about the many things I did wrong, but also the things that I did right. I will utilize my love of history as well to reference historical figures and examples of those who carved their own paths to success and significance.

I want you to see that it doesn't take superhuman talents or an Ivy-League education to live the life you have always dreamt of. It only takes a game plan.

At the end of the book, I have put together an organized, step-by-step guide that will allow you to create your own personal game plan. As you map out your life's path using these tools, you will become more adept at each step, ensuring you will be ready when opportunity comes.

CHAPTER 1

HARD LESSONS

I never let my schooling interfere with my education.
—Mark Twain (Samuel Clemens)

I couldn't agree more with Mr. Clemens, as my classroom education made up only the tip of the iceberg of knowledge I've acquired (and needed) on my journey. In fact, I am still collecting information every day. I read five books at a time. I listen to speakers on YouTube. I watch documentaries weekly. I spend hours on the phone each week asking people about their "why" and their "how." I have been fortunate enough in my career to be part of a rotating cast of hundreds and hundreds. With over 35 years in coaching, teaching, and speaking, I have found that there are certain habits and traits that led one farther down their path to success.

Of those 35 years, I have taught and coached at the high school level for 12 years, at the junior college level for one year, at the college level for 13 years, and spent the last 9 years of my coaching career in the National Football League. I have coached in the East (Knoxville, Tennessee), the West (University of Southern California), the North (Seattle, Washington), the Midwest (Dodge, Nebraska), the Mid-South (Blytheville, Arkansas, and Subiaco, Arkansas), and the South (Athens, Texas).

While the players at each of these schools and programs called me "coach," I would actually consider myself a professional watcher. That's what a coach is, right? We watch people do what we ask them to do and then attempt to praise or correct them based upon their performance of said task. You know the Tom Cruise movie *The Last Samurai*? It's like when he tells us that he is "surprised to learn that the term 'samurai' meant to serve." To me, the term "coach" actually means "to teach." As a teacher, I spend most of my time *observing* the habits and traits of each of my test subjects.

I have watched the healthy, wealthy, and wise, and I have watched the handicapped, downtrodden, and academically challenged find their way along their path. Each successful step (and each misstep) earned a mental notation on their scorecard. Some of them surprised me, but those who hit their markers and created solid habits were able to make steady progress down their life's path.

My unique study of success and failure has lasted 35 years. I can't think of a single study that has spanned that kind of period of time, can you? But here I am, having spent an incredible amount of time in the same industry watching the subjects go from the cradle to the grave, figuratively speaking, in the game of football. I have seen a young man put on his first football helmet—although it was backward—and I have seen a grown man weep after playing his last game of football. I have been part of winless seasons and historic runs of victories.

I have worked with geniuses (tested, in case you were wondering) as well as people who could not read above a third-grade level. I have studied people who came from every economic stratum imaginable. I have watched as those who were determined to succeed and willing to work and persevere achieved their goals, while others, who seemingly had everything going their way, squandered their talents and opportunities.

I really enjoyed watching how shared experiences affect each individual differently. How an individual coped with success or failure, how they fit into a team environment, and how they responded to discipline. To winning or losing. To competition. To being told the hard truth. To accepting the value of discipline. To learning how to handle pressure. Some responded by changing their habits to increase their chances of success, while others wanted to blame the people around them for their setbacks.

Using my 35 years of "research," I have come to an understanding of the key elements that enabled some to move smoothly down their path to significance, while others, who struggled with these tools, became stuck and were thus unable to keep moving down the line to see their hopes and dreams realized.

Over the scope of this book, I will choose the most important traits that enabled some to move on while the lack of these traits facilitated in an adverse outcome to their dreams. To begin to unpack some of these traits and habits, I want to start out by sharing three major pitfalls that I call "sticking points." These traits can stop a person dead in their tracks. They are:

1. Arrogance

2. Ignorance

3. Inflexibility

Three bullets that have killed many a career. While any one of these three sticking points can trip a person up, the biggest obstacle in moving past them is the individual himself. No matter how much someone wants to blame others for his troubles and his lack of success, often, the true villain in each of our stories is the person that looks back at us in the mirror every day.

Sticking Point #1: Arrogance

Let's start with the first of the terrible trio: Arrogance. Arrogance is defined by the Merriam-Webster dictionary as "an attitude of superiority manifested in an overbearing manner or in presumptuous claims or assumptions."

One of the common mistakes people make is that they confuse arrogance with confidence. Though a simple mistake, it's a deadly one. The minute we think we know everything, we soon learn how much we really don't know. I had to live this before I could understand it. It has taken me 35 years to understand the dangers that arrogance brings into the workplace. My first lab rat was, unfortunately, myself. I was *that* arrogant prick.

When I graduated from college, I felt I was as smart as any coach ever to join the profession. I could watch professional and college games on television and tell you all the ways the coach was screwing up. I could draw plays until I ran out of paper. If you can believe it, as I was looking for jobs, I wouldn't even apply for a position as an assistant coach. In my eyes, that was below me. Why would I sit there and work for a guy who couldn't know more than I did? So, I only applied for head coaching jobs.

During my interviews, I sold myself as a veteran coach, even though I had only coached a Little League baseball team when I was 16 years old. I had been reading biographies of coaches for years, so I had answers to their questions, and I knew football. From the time I could walk, football was part of my life. My mom was a huge Green Bay Packers fan. In the formal living room—the one with the plastic on the furniture and where we weren't allowed to go in when we were kids—there was a table that symbolized what was important in our household. On one end sat the Bible, and on the other sat Vince Lombardi's *Run to Daylight*. I had played organized football since the 3rd grade. I had collected football cards my whole life. Nate Low and I would play slow-motion football, reenacting all the plays we had watched on "Monday Night Football". In this regard, no one else had my resume… or so I arrogantly thought.

As it turned out, I did get the job at the high school, which proved that I was a much better salesman than I was a football coach. I was so prideful about what I thought I knew that I didn't know what I didn't know. I believed that if I just showed up, I would figure everything out. I was just fine in the weight room during the summer. Running plays with the kids after lifting went well.

But then the first day of practice, it was a shit show. I had no plan. But I still believed I was going to be able to bluster this thing through. I had two great assistants, Gordie Pilmore and Ken Ippenson. Both were good men, several years older than I was, and had coached longer than I had played the game. But I didn't ask for their advice. I was too busy looking for excuses for why things weren't going well.

The kids were great. They worked hard, and they listened. They performed what they were taught. As we sat on that bus heading home after getting beat… again… I had my first professional epiphany. It struck me like a thunderbolt.

I knew *nothing* about coaching the game of football.

When we have more confidence in ourselves than we do actual ability, it makes us difficult to be around. Now, don't get me wrong: there is nothing wrong with confidence. In a couple of chapters, I will discuss how the need to trust ourselves is essential to moving up in our world. However, when the confidence isn't backed up with the skill to prove it, you have a professional death sentence on your hands.

If we refuse to acknowledge our arrogance, we will become stuck. Once we're stuck, we will stagnate, and then we'll watch our professional aspirations start to die.

Now, this probably sounds either frightening or familiar. You see, as young people, our aspirations are sky-high. We dream of "the perfect life." It's easy to dream at this age because we don't understand the *cost* of our dreams. As we get older, our dreams begin to have some of the gilding knocked off as we begin to count the cost. Eventually, we move out on our own, and all too often, our dreams are put on hold because more important things have moved to the forefront. A roof over our head, food on our table, car payments,

> **If we refuse to acknowledge our arrogance, we will become stuck.**

insurance, children, a comfortable lifestyle we aren't willing to sacrifice, and the list goes on.

As the years go on and the bills get bigger, we begin to stagnate in our current situation. We can't leave, but we aren't moving up because that would call for sacrifice. We might have to move. Our work hours may change. Commitment to the job may become bigger than the commitment to the family. So, we stay stuck and stagnant.

Eventually, we become part of the furniture—always there. Younger people are moving through the system, and we are left behind. The only thing we have to look forward to is getting the gold watch. And 50 years later, they bury us… all because we refused to take the risk and make the changes that were required. This might sound extreme, but let me tell you: It's real.

I could have stayed at the high school and become a better football coach there. But a "good high school football coach" wasn't what I aspired to be, and it motivated me. After just one year in my first job, I resigned. I now understood that I needed to learn how to become a better coach. So, I took an offer from one of my college coaches and became an assistant so that I could learn the game of football and the profession of coaching. I decided that I needed to keep moving forward, avoiding being "stuck" at all costs.

And you can, too.

Sticking Point #2: Ignorance

While arrogance is a dream killer, I'd say that an even bigger threat is ignorance. And I'm not the only one to feel that way. Here is what Dr. Martin King, Jr. had to say in his book *Strength to Love* about ignorance: "Nothing in all the world is more dangerous than sincere ignorance and conscientious stupidity." To be clear, ignorance is defined by the Merriam-Webster dictionary as "the lack of knowledge, education, or awareness."

While I may now have been smart enough to know that I didn't know anything about coaching, I was still acting the same way I had in my first job when I took on the assistant position. In fact, I was able to help that team not win a single game the whole year. That's right: 0 – 10. Though I had dropped *some* of the arrogance by taking a supposed demotion to assistant, and I did learn how to plan a practice and the X and O stuff from the staff that I had joined, I didn't change the way I went about my work. This refusal to change was a huge sticking point in my movement through the profession.

I refused to give up my ignorance for the sake of gaining knowledge. Let me explain.

I was given the title "designated yeller." I wore it with pride, like a person sitting in the corner wearing a dunce cap thinking it was actually a crown. The players were always looking forward to the second day of two-a-days because I yelled so much during the first day, I lost my voice. I thought my bully tactics were the greatest tool in getting young people to respond. Intimidate them into excellence.

The staff that went O-fer split up that year, and I was taken in by the new head coach, Mickey Billingsley, as he put his staff together. As we prepared for the next season, I was taught a new system of play-calling on both the offensive and defensive sides of the ball. I still thought I was as smart as any coach on the staff and, truth be told, as smart as any we played against (or that I watched on TV). Yeah, I was a piece of work.

My thinking I was a football savant all changed when the coaching staff under Billingsley headed down to Little Rock, Arkansas, for the High School Coaches Clinic. This annual get-together was where the state high school coaches association would bring in successful coaches from around the country. The four-day extravaganza included speakers from high school, college, and professional teams.

The previous year was my first opportunity to attend this annual get-together. I was excited to match wits with coaches from other schools and to see how far ahead of the curve I really was.

I was tremendously disappointed. The keynote speaker, whose team had won the National Championship in college football the previous year, was 30 minutes late. When he did arrive, he stood up in front of the group and told two jokes that would get you fired if you told them in a mixed setting. He ended his talk abruptly, saying, "This is my offensive coordinator—he knows all the answers. I have to get out of here."

And that he did.

"I know you all came to hear Coach, so it won't hurt my feelings if you leave," The OC said as he took the stage. And wouldn't you know it, half the auditorium got up and left. Of course, I was one of them. I came to listen to a proven genius, not some sidekick. As I passed the hotel bar, I came across the head football coach who "had to leave." He was sitting in a booth with a few other old coaches, drinking whisky and telling stories.

I wasted an entire day that I could have been on the golf course with the rest of the coaches. Instead, I thought I might learn something. This won't happen again, I thought.

When the time came to go to Little Rock with Coach Billingsley's staff, I came prepared.

I brought my golf clubs.

Now, to clarify, I am *not* a good golfer. I once had my golf game analyzed by Bill Ryan, a fellow coach. He said, "What you need to do is to stop playing for two weeks…"

I leaned in, thinking this was all about overthinking the game and trying too hard. Then he continued: "…and then sell your clubs."

To go golfing when I could be learning was *not* something that I needed to do.

> **What you need to do is to stop playing for two weeks…**

That conference day, we had a 2:00 p.m. tee time. Bo Schembechler, the Hall of Fame head football coach at the University of Michigan, was the keynote speaker. He was scheduled to start speaking at 1:00 p.m., so I decided to stop in to give ole Bo a quick listen before I tore up some fairways (literally, I tore up divots of manicured sod the size of beaver pelts). As I stood in the back so I could make a quick getaway, I noticed that Joe Paterno (Penn State head football coach), Tom Osborne (University of Nebraska head football coach), and Eddie Robinson (Grambling State head football coach) were also in attendance.

If you don't know these men, they are some of the most iconic football coaches in the history of college football. All three had changed the game during their careers. They were what the 500 high school coaches in attendance aspired to be.

The difference between these three men and me was that I was standing in the back, and they were sitting in the front row with their pens and notebooks in hand. The best in the business were preparing to get better while I was preparing to stay the same.

Coach Schembechler began speaking at 12:58 p.m. and finished his two-hour talk at 3:00 p.m. I missed my tee time that day. Instead of terrorizing a golf course and the surrounding community, I found a seat—in the *front row* of the auditorium. The keynote speaker utilized every second of his allotted time speaking about his philosophy and fundamentals. He was kind and gracious when answering questions, asking each coach who raised his hand what his name was and what school he was associated with. Sure enough, he had recruited a kid from their schools at one time or another and had a story about the visit or the athlete.

To this day, if you want to find me in the audience of a coaching clinic, you will find me in the front row, right side, seated 20 minutes before the speaker starts. My run of ignorance ended that day, and I replaced it with a lifelong love of learning and zeal for knowledge. If those legendary coaches had taken the initiative to continue their education, then so could I.

This doesn't just occur in clinics. My bookshelves are full of my notebooks from every coaching staff meeting, team meeting, and position meeting that I attended for my entire career, from that clinic to today. Some of those amazing teachers and their messages found in my notebooks were:

Sherman Smith, running backs coach with the Seattle Seahawks, once started a meeting by wishing everyone a Happy Thanksgiving…

but it was in October. His message was that we should be thankful for all the things in our life every day, not just on one day in November.

Kris Richard, defensive coordinator with the Seahawks, once spoke to the team about the pain of discipline or the pain of regret. No matter what, you are going to have to suffer some sort of pain; the choice is yours.

Bill Russell, NBA legend, once spoke about loving everyone on your team, no matter what. He said that when we could do this, we would truly become a team.

Clint Bruce, former Navy SEAL and NFL football player, taught us about the stages to become elite. The middle stage was average, and he said, "Average has no secrets."

The best part about all these men? I didn't need to travel to listen to them share their scars. I would have been crazy not to borrow and utilize everything that came out of their mouths. I encourage you to look at *your* world. Where are the legendary speakers in your life or sphere? Maybe someone you have taken for granted is speaking during a lunch-hour seminar. How difficult would it be to bring your lunch to the auditorium and listen? We all have something to learn. Now, if you're making the excuse that you don't have the opportunity to have these people speak to you, I beg to differ!

Average has no secrets.

When I'm not out speaking, I will find great speakers on YouTube or read books that help me re-center myself. I am especially fond of speakers and authors who present a different philosophy than what I am currently working on. It might be as simple as a liberal watching Fox News or a conservative watching CNN, a Christian reading the Koran, or a Muslim reading the Bible. To understand an opposing viewpoint, you need to understand the lenses that they are speaking from. Only then can we hope to lose some of the ignorance that we shackle ourselves to.

To only read and listen to information that supports your current path is what Dr. King is speaking about when he says, "Sincere ignorance and conscientious stupidity." You must constantly fight to keep your mind open to useful information. But you must also be able to understand when someone is selling you (or those around you) a bad idea full of gimmicks and half-truths. This is part of your constant move away from ignorance and arrogance.

I do need to warn you, though. Once you take this path of learning, it can be overwhelming.

You may find that you are wrong. Oh, the horror! I think one of the greatest revelations we can gain is the understanding that everything we think we know may not be right. We may have been given the *Reader's Digest* format. But reeducation is more valuable than education that takes you farther from the path of truth. If we are unwilling to amend our ways, we may eventually be forced to make life-altering changes.

Learning to Learn

In November of 1997, I was the offensive line coach *and* strength coach at a junior college in Texas. The team was led by Scotty Conley, who gave the shortest, yet greatest halftime speech in the annals of college football when he said, "Snow just lost. WHEN we win, we will be in the National Championship game!" The players burst out of the locker room and beat their opponent that day. A week later, we would go on to win the JUCO National Championship.

After winning, I received a phone call from my mentor in strength and conditioning, the great John Stucky. He asked me if I was done with all the football coaching stuff, and if I was, if I would join him as a strength coach at the University of Tennessee. Which, of course, I jumped at.

When I got to Knoxville, John told me that he wanted me to become the "guru of football speed." I became familiar with speed development training when I had worked for Coach Stucky at the University of Arkansas. One of my areas of coaching was to train the Tennessee Volunteer football team in speed dynamics. Becoming the "guru" enabled me to travel around the country, soaking in the teaching methodologies from all of the greatest speed coaches in football and track. My mentor in speed was the great sprint coach Vince Anderson. I also learned from Mike Woicik, Tom Shaw, Al Miller, Loren Seagrave, Steve Javorek, and several others.

I took the initiative to call and visit each of these coaches. I watched them work and listened to their words, their cues, their nomenclature, and their body language to help them teach. Vince Anderson taught me how to watch film and what "perfect" looked like, picking out all the correct points so that when I saw "imperfect" in a real-life setting, the flaw would stand out. Vince was very patient with me. I sat for hours in his office watching athletes run, reading over his notes, and watching him work with sprinters. I then took this encyclopedia of information that I had learned with Vince on the road with me. The other football guys like Mike Woicik, Tom Shaw, and Al Miller helped to edit my newly gained knowledge to that which pertained, specifically, to football players.

Here is the problem. As I learned the answer to one question, five more questions grew out of the answer I received: the hydra effect. This name is derived from a mythological beast who grew five more heads after the one on its neck got cut off. Who would have guessed that I, once on the path to knowing everything there was to know about speed and training great athletes, would discover there may be no end? But that's the cool thing; there doesn't have to be a foreseeable end. It's the idea that chasing the elusive end is more fulfilling than, sometimes, finding the answer.

Sticking Point #3: Inflexibility

Thus far, I have told you stories about how I waded through my own swamp of arrogance and survived the desert wastelands of "sincere ignorance and conscientious stupidity." I must now help you find the way over the mountain of inflexibility. Inflexibility exists when one has a lack of interest or concern with the way they go about their work. People become apathetic when they believe that they aren't the problem, and because of that, they then have no desire to remedy the problem.

In the case of my own life, the blame game was strong. I couldn't see that I was the problem, and therefore, didn't care to change.

I had great men teaching me how to coach, including Mickey Billingsley and Letroy Gathan. In fact, these two men were two of the best coaches I had the great honor to watch throughout my career. They only used volume as a last resort. However, at the time, I was disinterested in seeing how they went about being successful. Instead, I was set in my own ways.

When the athletes I was working with didn't respond to my yelling, it wasn't my fault that they failed. I simply lacked any interest or concern in trying to learn another way. And dammit, I had to be right! I knew how to block a trap play seven ways from Sunday. I had yelled at my players every day leading up to the game, and when THEY didn't run the play correctly, I reasoned that there was no way it could've have been my fault. In my mind, I was the best coach on the field, so my thinking went, "It must be because the other coaches hadn't yelled as loudly as I did."

Inflexibility was the hardest and most painful (literally) of all the obstacles I had to face. My story in confronting my errant ways starts in a small farm community of around 600 souls. I had just gotten a job at Subiaco Academy, a boys' college prep school run by the Benedictine monks, located in the rolling hills of West Central Arkansas. I had just left the University of Arkansas, having earned my master's degree in history. However, I had received a doctoral-level learning experience in the weight room from John Stucky and his trusty sidekick, Tim Weiss. Subiaco would prove to be the laboratory for my training philosophy and program that would one day help teams and individuals win state, national, Olympic, and world championships.

In order to allow myself to grow, I needed to defeat the final of my three demons: inflexibility. To do this, I had to open my mind and face the truth. You may think that I "opened my mind" figuratively; however, in this case I actually had my mind opened for me via an industrial chicken house fan. If you didn't know, the 36-inch, stainless-steel blades on one of these fans can spin in excess of 1000 rpms. When I leaned in to find the on-and-off switch, I was struck with a vertical blow leaving a 6-inch opening from the middle of my forehead down below my left eye. Through God's grace, the fan blade jumped over my eye as it egg-shelled and crushed any bone that it came into contact with. I was (literally) so hard-headed that this didn't knock me down, nor did it knock me out. I was totally awake until getting put in a back of an ambulance because the attending doctor in the emergency room said, "He might not survive waiting for the Flight for Life helicopter."

I was in the hospital for a couple of weeks before they sent me home. After I had regained my strength and my recovery was coming along, I had just four weeks to get ready for the upcoming season. I was progressing well, and I felt better every day. Thankfully, the fog was clearing from my ravaged brain (from where the surgeon had to pick shards of my skull after they tore through the brain sack). I was taking a medication that was designed to keep the swelling down in my brain, but it was hindering my ability to watch game film. I used to have the ability to watch a play on the screen with five people moving at once and be able to critique each person on what went right or wrong. Now, I was having to watch each play five times to see what five people were doing. Not very time efficient. But I was determined to make it work. I figured the harder I worked, the better it would get.

It didn't, but that's not the lesson here.

The hardest blow hit when I went to my neurosurgeon so he could sign off on me getting back on the field for the beginning of two-a-days. He had a litany of dos and don'ts. He told me that I couldn't have any forceful physical contact. *Check.* I needed to eat right and drink right, which meant no alcohol and to get good sleep. *Check.* And finally, he said, "You can't strain."

"What do you mean by 'strain'?" I asked.

"You can't hold in a sneeze."

Doing so would cause intracranial pressure, which would kill me. *Check.* You can't lift weights. Doing so would cause intracranial pressure, which would kill me. *Check.* And finally, you can't yell. *Che…* Huh? Doing so would cause intracranial pressure, which would kill me.

If you remember, yelling was the primary tool in my "coaching toolbox." I grew up watching Vince Lombardi, Woody Hayes, and Bobby Knight. These three men had two things in common. One, they were very successful, and two, they yelled. This was the coaching method that I had brought with me from my first job, my second job, my graduate assistantship at the University of Arkansas, and now in my third job.

It wasn't just my tool of choice—it was my ONLY tool. I could intimidate an athlete very quickly with my yelling. I had been inflexible in my refusal to adapt my teaching style. I had no desire to initiate the change. My arrogance had been replaced by confidence, and my ignorance was being replaced with knowledge. But I had stubbornly stood firm on my coaching method, refusing to admit I was wrong.

The dynamics had changed. If I yelled now, it would cause intercranial pressure, which would kill me.

Now, I am not an overly religious man. I believe in a supreme being. I was brought up in the Catholic church, and like Bruce Springsteen said in his Broadway show, "They get you young, and they get you good." I have some background to tell, and if you will bear with me as I crawl up on the pulpit, I would like to throw some of my theological voodoo your way. I believe God nudges us along our paths. He allows for free will. But when we keep making the same stupid mistakes and

> **It wasn't just my tool of choice—it was my ONLY tool.**

have shown no signs of changing, he treats you like a stupid animal and rolls up his newspaper and hits you across the nose. In my case, the newspaper came in the form of a chicken house fan. And it did its job. I had to change. Or it would cause… I get it… Check!!

At this point, I could speak in no louder than a loud whisper—much like your mom would use in church when you were acting up with your siblings. I saw no way this was going to work. This was my first opportunity coaching these kids. How would they respect me if they weren't afraid of me? However, I started practice, and something scary happened. When I spoke, the athletes leaned in to listen. They didn't reel back in fear like I was used to.

Turns out, I did some of my best coaching that year. I found that when athletes wanted to listen, they would do what it takes. I had to make every word count. I also cleaned up my delivery with the practice field sitting in the shadows of the monastery and the steeples of the Catholic church. It wasn't the fear that made them better; it was their desire to learn. They responded much more to the *tone* than the volume that I was using, and they responded completely differently than with the giant hammer I had used in past. The sledgehammer that had not brought many victories, if we're being precise.

I was reminded of this lesson later in my life when I was coaching at the University of Southern California. The all-time great legend at USC, John McKay, made what would be his final visit to the practice fields. His time was nearly up as he shuffled to midfield. The team of players, coaches, trainers, and visitors all huddled around him. As he began to talk, his voice was less than a whisper. One hundred fifty heads leaned in to hear Coach McKay, and you could hear a pin drop in a pillow factory, it was so quiet. He spoke about his love for the university and the pride he had in the accomplishments of that team. And everyone listened intently because they wanted to hear him, and they wanted to learn.

Though he was barely audible, everyone heard everything he said. These kinds of voices are around us all the time, urging us to initiate change—to continue our movement from who we are to who we want to be. The voice each of us has can rally support or bring about change. The trouble in this world is that too few people are willing to lean in and listen and to accept the hard lessons as learning experiences. To lean into the lessons that they don't want to hear but that need to be heard.

That one "nudge"—finding my teaching voice in place of the bully voice—initiated a change in my path. From that job into my next four opportunities, I was able to motivate and train athletes, coaches, and teams to compete at the highest level and to live their best lives.

Be the Best

When I was working at USC as the strength and conditioning coach, we had the worst weight room in all of college football. In fact, one time, Nick Saban and Urban Meyer were on campus to shoot an ESPN promo for the upcoming season. They had no sooner stepped in the shoebox with leaking ceilings and rusty pipes overhead when they asked where the football weight room was. I shrugged and said, "Well, this is it, as well as the weight room for the other 19 sports." Both laughed and said they were going back to their respective schools to get on the strength coaches who told them that they needed all the bells and whistles to compete!

I could have sat there and complained about the condition of the weight room with the lack of space and water that would leak through the ceiling when they watered the plant boxes on the patio above. But it wouldn't have gotten us closer to being a championship program. I liked the rough gym, and it didn't hurt us in recruiting. We didn't need flashy walls and pictures to pick up and put down weights. We only needed to be motivated to push ourselves from where we were to where we wanted to be.

Look at where you are now and rejoice because that is precisely where you initiate your ascent to success. If you are in the mailroom, be the greatest mailroom person in the world. If you are a junior executive, don't wish for that bigger job; find out how you can help change your company to a better company. When you make *your* world better, they will come find you.

I've only had one job interview in my life. It landed me my first job, and after that, my reputation got me the next one. I can tell you a bunch of stories about coaches who wasted their time looking for the next thing and missed out on doing their best at their current job—which would have catapulted them to positions they had only dreamt of.

After you have gotten out of your own head and understand that you are actually in the best place possible, then you need to go out and learn how to make yourself (and the work you do) better. I had an old coach once tell me that he would always have a job.

"How's that?" I asked.

"I'm the only one who knows how to turn on the water for the fields." He found his niche, that one thing that allowed him to continue to be who he wanted to be. Find out what makes your company tick—where the watering system is—and become the best and most knowledgeable person at doing *that* job.

If you aren't sure where that one thing is, don't be afraid to ask questions of the people above and around you. It's not a stupid question if you don't know the answer; it's only stupid if you don't ask the question.

I once was walking through the meeting rooms when I was at the University of Tennessee when I saw that one of the rooms had a video playing. As I peeked in the room, I found Peyton Manning—who had just been chosen as the first pick in the first round of the NFL draft—watching the same play over and over and over again. He looked over from his study, and I took my chance.

"Whatcha doin'?"

"I'm looking for this guy's give."

A "give" is a telltale sign that would expose a player's true intentions, and he was watching for the give of an NFL player that the Colts would be playing that season. He must have watched that one guy for most of an hour to find the answer. Later on, he was walking through the weight room, and I asked him if he found it. He smiled and said, "It was his left shoulder."

And that's why Peyton was so special. He found the answer no matter how long it took him. And that's how I got smarter—I wasn't afraid to ask him a "stupid" question.

"Whatcha doin'?"

Which One Are You?

When I lived on Pine Crest Drive in Chadron, Nebraska, my best friend was a guy named Doug Ross. We were together an awful lot. Whether it was shooting BB guns on Cassidy Hill, a sandstone outcropping behind my house, or at his house playing with his Johnny West action figures, we always had a great time. Doug always wanted to be a cowboy. But I always wanted to play football.

My family moved away from Chadron when I was going into the 3rd grade in 1970. Eleven years later, I moved back to Chadron after receiving a football scholarship offer at Chadron State College. My second night back in town, I was at Herman's, a bar in the middle of the town. I was talking with some other guys that were on the football team when I was tapped on the shoulder. I turned to see this scrappy little guy with a big mustache wearing a cowboy hat.

"What's up?" I asked.

"You don't recognize me?"

I shrugged and said, "I can't say as I do." Remember, this is long before cell phones and Instagram. When you moved away, it was easy to lose contact with people you might have known when you were 7 or 8 years old. The wiry cowboy smiled broadly and said, "It's me, Doug Ross."

He grew up to be the cowboy he always wanted to be, and I had grown up to play football. Funny how life works out sometimes. We spent the rest of the night talking and laughing.

Sometime later, I walked into the 120 Bar and saw Doug sitting at the bar talking to an older gentleman. This guy was an OG cowboy—from the hat that sat on the bar to his well-worn cowboy boots, the faded Wranglers, the round circle on the back pocket that denoted the location of his can of Copenhagen, the denim shirt, and the kerchief around his neck. His face was like an old leather glove. Every crease was a story that he had earned. His hands were the hands of a grinder, one that has given every ounce of himself to his passion—living the life of a cowboy.

Doug introduced me, and we sat and talked for what seemed like forever. I sat on one side of the old cowboy, and Doug was on the other. I noticed it was getting late, so I looked into the clear-blue eyes of my new friend and said, "I've got time for one more. Give me your best story."

He smiled at me and took a drink of his beer, slid another dip into his lip, and got to it.

"An Eastern newspaper reporter was riding along to get the feeling of what it would be like to ride on a cattle drive. After the first day of riding, the reporter dismounted and watched one of the cowboys. The first thing the cowboy did as he dismounted his horse was complain about his place on the ride. He was riding in the back of the herd, or in the 'trail position.' He pulled the saddle off his horse and put it in place near the fire. He then headed to the chuck wagon to get something to eat before anyone else could get there. After he had eaten, he pulled his blanket off his saddle and rolled over to go to sleep.

"The next morning, the reporter watched him again. He was the last one to get out of his bedroll, and he immediately started complaining about how hard the ground was. When he got to the coffee pot, it was down to the bottom. As you can imagine, the cowboy complained about how cold the coffee was and then asked the foreman if he could change positions, maybe up to the lead.

"The foreman chuckled and sent him back to the back of the herd.

"The reporter decided to ride with the cowboy and ask him questions. The cowboy didn't even wait for the first question before he started complaining. He complained about his flea-ridden, broken-down horse, moaning about having to ride in the back and eat the dust all day. If a steer strayed away from the herd, he acted like he didn't see it, forcing one of the other cowboys in the trail to bring it back to the herd. Not only did he complain about everything under the sun, but he topped it off by doing the least amount of work that he could.

"The reporter was able to work a single question into the monologue of complaints. The reporter asked, 'What will you do with your pay when you get to the end of the trail?'

"The cowboy smiled and said, 'I'm going to drink and gamble. And when I sober up, I'm going to hook up with another company.'

"When they finished riding that day, the reporter decided to watch another one of the cowboys. After the ride, the second cowboy tied up his horse and took off his saddle. The foreman told him to go get water for the company at a nearby stream. After getting the water, the second cowboy ate dinner while he talked to some of the other cowboys around the fire, sang some songs, and then went to bed. The next day, this cowboy got up, sipped a warm cup of coffee, and got his horse ready for the day. The foreman appreciated his work from the past day, so he moved him up to riding wing, which meant he would be riding alongside the herd, keeping the cattle hemmed in.

"The reporter spoke to the second cowboy as they traveled. He asked him how he liked being a cowboy. The cowboy smiled and said it was good work, and he enjoyed being with his friends.

"'What are you going to do with your pay?' the reporter asked.

'I'm going to go to the bank and deposit half of it, then take the other half and go to get a good dinner, have a drink or two, and maybe play some cards. One day, I would like to become the foreman of a cattle ranch.'

"At the end of the day, the reporter decided to watch a third cowboy. As soon as the cowboy got to camp, he tied up his horse, took off the saddle, watered the horse, and began to wipe it down. After that, he brushed his horse until it shined like a show pony. Finally, he checked the horse's hooves, making sure they had no issues or a stone hadn't gotten stuck in the shoe. When he had finished with his horse, he walked past the chuckwagon and asked the cook if he could do anything to help. The cook asked if he could get him some more water, which he gladly did. When the third cowboy got back, he was happy to find that the cook held out a choice piece of meat, some beans, and bread for him. He and the cook ate dinner together, laughing at the songs being sung by the fire. After eating, the third cowboy offered to help the cook wash the dishes that had been used by the rest of the men.

"After finishing the dishes, the third cowboy noticed the foreman was saddling his horse on his nightly ride around the herd. He asked the foreman if he could ride the herd with him to check on everything, and the foreman was glad to have the company. When the cowboy returned about an hour later, he again watered his horse, wiped it down, brushed it, checked its shoes, fed it, and headed toward the fire. By the time he settled down, everyone had been sleeping for a while.

"When dawn broke, the reporter awoke to the smell of coffee. As he sat up and stretched, he noticed it was the third cowboy who had taken on the responsibility of getting the coffee ready for the company. That day, the foreman put the third cowboy in the lead position. The cowboy worked hard that day. He was moving around the herd, helping each of the groups as they needed it. He found a shallow fording spot across the river, which saved the drive several hours. As they drove the cattle into the railhead, the reporter asked the cowboy if he could ask him some questions.

"The cowboy said it would have to be quick because the cattle company had recognized his talents and had given him a promotion to cattle agent. The train was heading out within the hour.

"'What are you going to do with your pay?' the reporter asked.

"The cowboy chuckled and said he was going to put all of the money in the bank.

"With that, the cowboy started to ride away. The reporter asked one last question: 'What do you hope to do one day?' The cowboy turned in his saddle and said, 'One day, I will own all of this land and all of the cattle on it.' And he rode away to his next opportunity."

The old cowboy got up to leave and said, "Three different cowboys—all doing the same work, all getting the same pay. Which one are you?"

> **Three different cowboys—all doing the same work, all getting the same pay. Which one are you?**

Know Your *Who*

That cowboy's question was asked of me almost 40 years ago, and I still think about it today, measuring myself off what the old man had told me. I have to separate myself from who I *think* I am, who I am *perceived* to be, and who I *actually* am. I can see where this might be hard to understand.

1. My ego sees me as the third cowboy, of course—the guy who is hungry to get better.

2. I may be perceived as any of the three cowboys. This is dependent upon your perception of how I am received in our daily interactions.

3. Upon deeper analysis, we're probably not as good as we think we are, yet we are not as bad as some perceive us to be. In truth, we likely have aspects of all three cowboys.

With this in mind, I ask myself the following questions (and encourage you to do the same): How close am I to becoming the first cowboy, with no redeemable qualities? Or the second cowboy, who was just doing the job that was in front of him?

I *always* strive to be the third cowboy—the one who thought of others before himself. Have I looked to lend my talents and abilities to lighten the load of those who were burdened with more than they could handle? Have I looked for opportunities to learn more about the process as the third cowboy had done by riding with the foreman, when it would have been easier to lie down or sing around the fire with the other guys? Am I investing in my future to be able to get to where I one day want to be, or am I living for the moment, giving the future away?

I now ask you the same question that the old cowboy had asked me. *Which one are you?*

Take a minute to mull over the three examples presented in the old cowboy's story. You need to be truthful with yourself now, and you need to own the answer. I'm not asking you which one you would *like* to be. Not the one that you are perceived to be by others. I want you to step back and truthfully own which description fits who you are *right now*.

Are you the kind of person that complains all the time? Always asking to be given more responsibility when you haven't earned the responsibility you've already been given? The one who only thinks of themselves and their creature comforts?

If you see yourself wavering between each of the examples, what can you do to get as far away from the first cowboy as possible?

Maybe you are somewhere in between the first and the second cowboys. Are you the person who just does the job you are asked to do, yet complains when you are passed up for promotions? One who is dependable to do what has been asked but will not stretch yourself to do or initiate something new? Unless, of course, it benefits you in some way or another? You are liked by all, and that is important to you. You don't want to miss out on a good time.

Are you the person who is always busy being productive? The one who cares for those around you? The one who is making the organization better? Are you built for the long run? Are you committed to your success, not only financially, but with every beat of your heart, with every breath you take?

To make sure we are on the same page as far how I am using the term "committed," I love tennis great Martina Navratilova's quote differentiating between "committed" and "involved."

"The difference between involvement and commitment is like ham and eggs. The chicken is involved; the pig is committed."

So, I ask again: Are you committed in your quest to live the life that you have always dreamt you could live? Or is this a passing whim, something you would like to be involved in, something that, as long as it fits your schedule and doesn't take too much effort, you might like to look into?

As we ponder these questions and this story, we can begin to create our "who." We can begin to grow from the person we *were* to the person we *want* to be. We want to move from the person who was not getting us where we wanted to be—the one who got us stuck and allowed us to stagnate—to the person who will take us beyond our wildest dreams. That person is inside of us, and they are the one we know we can become.

> **The difference between involvement and commitment is like ham and eggs. The chicken is involved; the pig is committed.**
> **—Martina Navratilova**

I would love to give you a few examples of these types of people from history. Fortunately, no one builds monuments, erects statues, or writes books about people who never accomplished anything. The reason why is that, going back to what my friend Clint Bruce so clearly told us, "Average has no secrets."

Not many people are interested in being average. Average is easy—you just wake up and get out of bed. However, if you wanted to continue to live the life you are living, I suspect you wouldn't have picked up this book.

If you take the steps to change the trajectory of your life now, one day, they might fill libraries with your stories. Orville and Wilbur Wright dreamt one day they would fly. They were not classically trained in aeronautics, but they figured it out. A bicycle repairman and a printer figured out the issues with flight. Oprah Winfrey changed her life, fighting through her early struggles to become one of the most influential people in the world. If any of these people had settled for mediocrity, do you think we would even know their names, let alone honor them for their ingenuity and struggles?

Preparation

I thought I was going to be happy winning championships in football. So, I did that. But I still wasn't fulfilled. It took long periods of introspection to figure out why I wasn't satisfied—what I was actually destined to do and be. It wasn't the winning that I craved, though it's a hell of a lot better than the alternative. It was the process of helping people find their path to significance, helping people attain their goals and become the person they were always meant to be.

Whether it was the athletes or students I worked with daily, my main goal was to help them overcome whatever was holding them back. When they inevitably failed, I was there to help them pick up the pieces, retool, and prepare for the next effort. When they were successful, I stepped back and let them enjoy the moment. After the confetti fell to the floor and the party hats were put away, I was there to help them with whatever came next.

As you work through the process of truly understanding who you are and what you need to do to become who you expect yourself to be, let me remind you what set the third cowboy apart. It can be summed up in one word: Preparation.

What was the *first* thing that the third cowboy did when he got off his horse at the end of the day? He prepared his most important commodity for the *following* day: His horse. Without his horse, he was useless.

You must prepare for tomorrow by setting yourself up for success the night before. Put your clothes out, making sure they are clean and appropriate for who you want to be. Do you desire to be a top-level business executive? You'd better dress the part!

Before you leave for the day, make sure your desk is ready to go for the next and check your daily planner for anything coming up. Before you go to bed, set two alarms—one that is battery-operated in case your phone or alarm clock loses power overnight. That alarm should allow you to get to work an hour before you need to be there. If you are early, you can get ahead. Again, make sure you set out the clothes you will wear for the person you *want* to be, not the person you are *presently*. If you aspire to be in upper management, then invest in clothes that make you look like the people who hold the job you want. If you want to be on a marketing team and all of the members look like they are Brooks Brothers catalogue models, and you wear sandals and blue jeans, the head of marketing will likely gloss right over you. Once you get on the team and show your worth, then you can go back to wearing your comfortable clothes. But at that point, you may not want to go back…

When I attended a staff meeting, I would wear different clothes than I did when working with the athletes. Now, don't get me wrong; I wouldn't put on khakis and a polo shirt, but I *would* put on a clean pair of shorts and shirt and a nice pullover. Although I wasn't in my domain, I needed to blend in with the rest of the staff so that my message wasn't drowned out by my field attire.

Build a Bridge

The next thing the third cowboy did was ask if he could help the cook, which, again, we can learn an immense amount from.

When you are finished with the work on your desk, can you lend a hand to someone who may be overwhelmed? When you reach out and ask if other people need help, they see you as a team player. If someone asks you for help, make sure the job is done better than it has ever been done before so your name will be passed on to other people who want ambitious, hard workers!

This is all part of building bridges. In the story, imagine the cook telling the trail boss all about what a hard worker the third cowboy is, which leads to the trail boss elevating the third cowboy to the front of the herd, rather than keeping him in the back eating dust the whole day. In the end, the third cowboy got an immediate payment for his help. His meal was kept warm, and he earned another ration of beef.

A good friend of mine, Ben Malcolmson, is a prime example of this happening in real life. In his book *Walk On,* he describes his ascent from a college sports reporter who did a "George Plimpton" (going from the position of sportswriter to being on the team). He continued to show his value in different positions inside the organization until he ended up being the right-hand man for one of the most powerful football coaches in the business. Ben is a *master* at building bridges.

After dinner, the cowboy helped with the dishes. When I was in college, I took a class taught by the head football coach, Jerry Welch. He had two major points that he emphasized. The first was this: Don't burden your team with unnecessary rules. The second thing, which pertains to this subject, is to get to know the people who make the company move. These are the people like secretaries, custodial services, security, and the crew in the cafeteria. The lifeblood of the organization runs through these men and women. I am allergic to fish, so the head of the cafeteria, Mac McNabb, always made sure I steered away from those choices. He made my life easier by helping me avoid the potholes along my path, like a trip to the ER.

In the evening, the last thing the third cowboy did was to volunteer to do more work with the boss. This opportunity to be alone with someone in upper management is *invaluable.* These opportunities also help you learn about the overall operation. You see, every organization has a system in place to get the job done. As time goes on, the skilled professional finds shortcuts to get things done more efficiently. Not *more easily*, but more effectively. You simply cannot learn this stuff by just showing up. You need to be in the hip pocket of those who know more than you. As you become more familiar with the people above you, it will open lines of communication. It is a great time to ask a "stupid" question or two to show a person (who may not recognize your skills) that you are eager to learn.

Find a New Way

The following day, the third cowboy made sure he was the first one up. In your case, you'll be the first one at work so you can get a head start on what you have going for the day. You can punch up a presentation, or you can take your newfound knowledge and use it to make sure that you are a step ahead of others vying for the same job.

During the day, the third cowboy worked relentlessly. What you're doing for a living is not just your job—it needs to become your *passion*. Your days will fly by if you stay in the groove and keep working on your projects. A study once said that the average worker works less than four hours out of every eight-hour workday. Think of the amount of work you can get done if your work proficiency is twice that of the other people at your company! That is also twice the amount of work your competition is putting in.

The third cowboy didn't just ride along the way they always came; he found the alternate route. He didn't change how the cattle were herded, but by changing the direction that could be taken, in the end, he shortened the time the cattle were losing weight on the trail. This allowed the cattle company to make more money. As you find more ways to put work in and start to understand the inner workings of the organization, you can make strategic suggestions that can drastically change the success path of your company.

Too often, lower-ranking employees don't take the initiative to find better ways to do a task. They will continue doing things the same way because "that's the way it's always been done." You don't need to reinvent the wheel, but coming up with a workable plan that streamlines a part of the business, which then speeds up a process in the organization, can be your ticket to bigger opportunities.

The final thing the cowboy did was to continue to move up in the "company." Businesses will not serendipitously come to your office and pluck you out to do something more important if they haven't seen your work or your potential. The cowboy made it happen through his effort and focus. It didn't take an advanced degree. It didn't take years and years.

Companies want to make money, NOW. If you have shown them how important you are to the success of the company, they will want you in a leadership role. And then you simply follow the same steps to become the person necessary to be successful in that role.

Know Your *What*

So, who are you now? And who do you want to be? As you go through the process of answering these questions, you also need to become aware of your *what*. The "what" is the thing that will make a person different than all the others who are vying for the same position, the same golden ring at the carnival we call life.

When we look at the three cowboys, each one had the same abilities as the other two. However, it is the third cowboy who used all of his talents that would one day allow him to be successful.

When I was growing up, one of my favorite days of the year was when we went to pick up our school supplies from Target. I know this sounds odd, especially if you understand just how much I hated school, but I *loved* school supplies. Pencils, erasers, notebooks, pens, erasers, protractors, more erasers… I suppose I needed all of those erasers because I made, and still make, a lot of mistakes in the planning stages.

The most important thing for me was getting the right crayons. They had to be *Crayola* crayons. I couldn't deal with the off brand, though they were cheaper. I would always get the 8-pack of Crayola crayons. The 8-pack had every color that I would ever need. When I was growing up, these crayons were as thick as a grown man's thumb and much longer than the crayons that came in the normal pack. They were built for someone who was not going to go gently into a coloring book. These crayons were not for "fine art." These tools were not built to stay in the lines but to expand subjects to their farthest extent. In some sense, they were built to think outside the box—to discover how far one could take a given subject.

As you may remember, the choices of Crayola crayons expanded exponentially. From the trusty 8-pack, you could go to the 16-pack, 24-pack, 48-pack, 64-pack, or even the coveted 128-pack. Some of these boxes even had a built-in sharpener! But I didn't want the bigger boxes. You see, the biggest problem was that I was an intense "artist." When I colored an ocean, I would press so hard that the picture became three-dimensional from the layers of crayon I left on the page. The second reason I didn't like using those skinny crayons was that I was passionate about the task at hand, and a normal crayon would break under the pressure I applied. Only the thickest crayons would survive my heavy-handed coloring. Because of these reasons, my mom would describe me as a "grinder."

Grinders don't believe enough is really enough. They are only finished when there is nothing left. In this case, it was only when the whole picture (and the rest of the page) were covered with color. By the middle of the academic quarter, my crayons did not sit neatly in the box. In fact, the box was almost as worn out as the contents. The crayons were nothing but bits and pieces, and no paper remained. Just shrapnel, as if a crayon factory had exploded, and all that was left were tiny pieces.

I have lived my life a lot like I colored. I am intense, and many times, I've been so passionate it has bordered on being a zealot. There is no "quit" in me. I will continue on the task until I have finished what I set out to accomplish. After years and years of trying to be who I *wasn't*, I finally grasped who I was. I understood my talents and utilized them to their highest degree. I was not a head football coach. I was not an offensive coordinator. Like my limited number of crayons, I'm not as gifted as other people. But I use ALL of the talent that God has given me. When my time comes and the clock runs out, I will be nothing but a bunch of used up bits and pieces, bones and gristle, because I will not go "gently into the night."

With these "crayons," I helped people accomplish their greatest dreams. My intensity and passion can be seen in the physical product that dominated the playing fields in college and the NFL. I was only a cog in the machines, but I believe my work played a factor in the success. I used my talents to develop the athletes' abilities to match that which they would be called to perform on the playing field. Many of the players I worked with were already tremendous athletes. But there is a huge difference between being an athlete and being a finished football player.

Your crayons are your gifts and talents. They can be as diverse as Jackson Pollock is to Michelangelo or Vince Lombardi is to John Wooden. When you understand what you are best at, then you learn to live through your talents.

You may be blessed with the likes of the 128-pack of crayons with the built-in pencil sharpener. If you are, then use all of your talents. Use all of your crayons. When I was in elementary school, I found satisfaction when I looked at my nubs and scraps of crayons and saw the person sitting next to me who had all the same tools but didn't use them. There the crayons sat on their desk, all stacked neatly in the box with the same flat tip that the maker created them with. They could have done so much more, but they were satisfied with less.

Too many people have the talent to change this world into something better, but they hesitate. They get focused on just a few of their strengths, and they stop. They don't continue to test and try all of their crayons to find out how they all work together. Sure, the picture might seem unclear as you are figuring out how to use your talents, but eventually, you will start to see. If you never use your gifts, you will never maximize your true potential.

On the other side are those who could be likened to the 8-packs or even 64-packs and believe themselves to be more than they really are. They continue to grind, but the colors never coalesce into results.

I was that guy for the first 10 years of my career. I thought I was going to make my name as a great football coach. I was grasping at crayons that I had no idea how to use. Luckily for me, I had the epiphany that I wasn't a football coach. I was able to use my 8-pack to become the best strength and conditioning coach that I could possibly be.

Those who continue trying to be what they aren't have a specific category they fit into. It is called the "Peter Principle." This occurs when one climbs to the highest level of their incompetency. At this point, their career will stagnate. Pride won't let them say, "Yeah, I was a great assistant, but not a very good head coach." They continue to get hired in jobs that are out of their wheelhouse. Even though lightning may strike on their way up and they have a winning season or two, as they climb to larger opportunities, they can never live up to their best seasons—the ones that some saw as potential. In reality, those seasons were a confluence of good fortune all coming together at one time. Soon enough, this "potential" becomes the lead weight that drags them down the profession. Eventually, they are working in some backwater location trying to make one more run.

As I went through the process of trying to understand who I truly was and what my unique strengths were, I also reached outside of my crayon box. To learn more about my profession, I would read biographies by successful coaches like Bobby Bowden and Jimmy Johnson and think, *Hey, this is the "secret" to being successful. If I act like them and talk like them, I can be a successful football coach.*

The biggest difference between these guys and myself was that they understood their strengths better than I understood mine.

Instead of being me, I tried to emulate them. I tried to expand my crayon box. When I did, I became less effective as a coach because I didn't possess the skill to accomplish the job that needed to be done. Bowden and Johnson both understood something very important: They understood what their crayon box was lacking. These coaching legends would go out and select young, highly motivated and intelligent assistants. Each assistant brought his own crayons into the picture, which made for dominating football teams. It wasn't just Bobby Bowden or just Jimmy Johnson running the show; it was the people they brought with them who used their strengths to shore up the weaknesses.

In Bruce Springsteen's *VH1 Storytellers*, after the credits go by, there is a question-and-answer period. The first question is from a guy who leads in by talking about how Springsteen bares his soul when he sings. He throws out some of the titles of Bruce's songs and then says, "I feel like I know you. Do I?"

Without hesitation, Springsteen says, "No." Everyone laughs, and he goes on to say, "It's part of the job, the whole 'feel like I know you thing.'"

No matter how much we admire those people, we can't *be* them. The good news is that we can actually be *better* if we stay in our lane. Oscar Wilde tells us, "Be yourself; everyone else is taken." We all have our own crayons. If you think you want to be the next… whoever you want to be, you must know that they are who they are because they used their set of crayons. But here's the deal: There is already one of them! And there is only one of YOU. Change the game the way that J.K. Rowling did. Move the needle in the area that you are gifted in.

Rowling's strength was not in trying to emulate another author's style but in writing in *her* voice. *Harry Potter* was turned down by every literary company. Why? Because she didn't write like the other authors in her genre. But we all know what happened in the end! And now she's got a whole crop of new authors trying to emulate *her* style. She used her crayons. She understood who she was. She understood her talents and worked on her craft. And she believed in herself.

Steve Jobs also understood what his strengths were. They were not writing code or in the wiring of a computer; rather, he understood shape and symmetry. He had great vision for what the world was lacking and how he could fill that need. Was he right all of the time? Not always, but when he stayed in his lane, he would take his industry and reshape it in ways that no one else had ever considered. Whether

> **Be yourself; everyone else is taken.**
> **—Oscar Wilde**

it be in computers or animation, he changed the way that we now live and view future possibilities.

So, what are your crayons? What are your strengths and talents? How can you lean into them, and how can you find people who complement your weaknesses?

Not Using All Your Crayons

On the flip side of the people who try to use too many crayons—crayons that are not in their box—there are the people who never use the crayons they have at their disposal. Too many people have all this talent stored up, yet they only use two or three of their strengths.

The great artist Michelangelo is quoted as saying, "The greater danger for most of us lies not in setting our aim too high and falling short, but in setting our aim too low and achieving our mark." He is speaking to all of us. Too many people are satisfied with being unfulfilled, on being good at just one thing when their potential is so much more.

One of the most tragic occurrences of not using all of your talents came into my life early in my coaching career. I met Tony and Cathy when I was hired on to be the head football coach at their local high school. They were always there when we needed a helping hand. Whether it be painting the weight room, handing out equipment before camp started, decorating the locker room for homecoming, or cooking burgers for the team after the game in the rain, they were always the first to ask if we needed any help.

**The greatest danger
is setting our aim too low
and achieving it!
—Michelangelo**

Tony and Cathy had two sons, Mike and Rick. Mike was the older and played on my football team. Mike was a solid football player. He wasn't necessarily athletically gifted, but he made up for this with great effort and hustle. On the other hand, Rick was a member of the band and the honor society. This kid was special. He wasn't an athlete like his brother and his father, but he excelled in the classroom. Rick was a straight "A" student with a great gift in the area of math.

When Mike graduated from high school, he followed Tony's path and married his high school girlfriend and got a job at the local factory. He had no ambitions to go on to college and dreamt of one day being part of management at the factory, just like his dad. Now, let me be clear: There is nothing wrong with this. Tony and Mike were hitting on every cylinder. They were using all of their crayons.

Two years later, Rick graduated as the valedictorian of his class. I told you this kid was special! It took most of the graduation ceremony to read off the academic scholarship opportunities that he had been offered. Rick accepted the full scholarship grant from the largest in-state university, which was ranked in the top 10% in the country for math. The icing on the cake was that he and his longtime girlfriend could go to school together.

I was invited to Rick's wedding in the summer after his freshman year in college. Rick was excited about the opportunities that lay ahead of him. The professors at the university saw the potential in the young man and had already introduced him to some very powerful people in the corporate world.

Three years later, I received Rick's graduation announcement from Tony and Cathy. By this time, I had moved on to another opportunity and had lost touch with the four of them. That evening, I gave Tony a call to congratulate him and Cathy on raising such a great kid. Cathy answered the phone, and we talked about how proud they were of his accomplishments. Cathy told me that Rick had graduated at the top of his class. When Tony got on the phone, the first question I asked him was, "Where is Rick going to go to continue his education?"

Tony took on a low voice and said, "Don't start that talk, Coach. He needs to get a job and get on with his life."

I tried to paint the big picture of what *could* happen, but Tony had no desire to listen to what might be when he had already gotten

Rick a job on the factory line. He and Cathy had picked out a house near theirs that Rick and his wife were going to rent.

They had Rick's life planned out. They "let him" get all the college thing out of his system, and now it was time to get his 40 hours in and start giving them grandchildren. And Rick followed their plan. In my opinion, Rick was a difference maker. Had he allowed his life to continue to move in the direction it was moving, he would have changed the world. Rick didn't see problems; he saw solutions. He had a huge box of crayons. He could have been that elusive piece to some puzzle that made our world a better place.

Several years later, I was asked by the school to come back and speak at their sports banquet. The topic of my talk that night was "Taking Risks: Living Your Best Life." I thought it was appropriate with all of the seniors having finished their sporting careers. I challenged them to come "out of the blocks" chasing their dreams. To use all of their crayons to complete the picture of their life in a way that represented their having maximized their potential.

I spoke to Rick after my talk and asked, "How are you doing, *really*?" He smiled, then dropped his head and said, "I hope these kids heard your message."

I looked him in the eye and said, "Did you?" And with that, he gave me a big hug and walked away.

It's easy to sit here and say, "It wasn't all his fault; his parents pumped the 'get a job' narrative throughout his life." But it is wrong to think that just because his parents had their plans that Rick was innocent. It was still Rick's decision to not take a different path, the one less traveled "that made all the difference," to quote Robert Frost.

Too many times in life, we let other people take over our life's roadmap. Sometimes we get pigeonholed as not being good enough or not being worthy. Whether it be by family, friends, or in school, somewhere along the process a moment comes where someone shuts our box of crayons and says, "That's good enough."

We must always be aware of this happening around us… and we must start with ourselves. Are we shutting our kids' lives down because they have already exceeded *our* expectations? What if the reality is that their dreams are bigger and reach farther than we could ever comprehend? As influencers in our own spheres, do we understand the potential of the people around us? The simplest way that we can start to solve the problem of holding others back is through open communication. We need to find out what excites those around us and give them options. Ask them hard questions. Make them dig down deep to find out who they are and what do they really want to do.

Tony and Cathy didn't know of a different way. Neither had left their hometown. They were programmed into doing what they were taught. If I had done a better job as a friend, I might have helped Rick get to where he wanted to be. I still kick myself today for not working harder on behalf of Rick, for not trying to provide a clearer understanding of their son's potential.

Had I been farther along my own path of understanding, I would have used the story of my high school football coach to help them understand what could happen if Rick would be allowed to use all of his crayons.

Let me give you an example of a guy who used all his crayons during his illustrious career. He was never content with resting on his past successes, and he always knew he could achieve more. My high school football coach, Barry Alvarez. In 1978, he led a bunch of kids from Mason City, Iowa, to the AAAA High School State Championship. He could have shut his crayon box right there and stopped his career path and stayed in Mason City for the rest of his life talking about that championship game. But he didn't. He went on to be a linebacker coach at the University of Iowa and then the defensive coordinator at Notre Dame, where his defense helped the Fighting Irish win a college football National Championship. He could have stopped at either of these stages in his coaching career, and he would have accomplished more than most. But he didn't. From Notre Dame, he moved on to be the head coach at the University of Wisconsin for 16 years. In 2010, he was voted into the college football hall of fame. He could have stopped anywhere along the line. He could have put his crayon box on the shelf. But he continued to strive for more and more, changing countless people's lives along the way.

At a retirement press conference in 2021, he was asked, "If someone had told when you first started out coaching all that you would accomplish, would you be surprised?" His answer was simple. "No, I always knew what I wanted to do with my life. All that was a mystery was where it would all happen."

Coach Alvarez kept hitting his mark and resetting the target farther and farther, using every one of his crayons along the way. His influence and that of his offensive line coach at Mason City, Ed Lenius, changed my life. Together, these two men made me to want to become a coach so that I could have a positive effect on others' lives. Following their example of striving for and obtaining success and bringing people with them on their path is something that I knew I wanted to do in my own life.

> No, I always knew what I wanted to do with my life. All that was a mystery was where it would all happen.

Know Your *Why*

When we understand our *Who* and our *What*, we can finish the picture by working on our *Why*. This is the hardest one. The "why" is this: Why are you willing to go through the reconstruction of your life to accomplish your dreams? The work thus far has all been mental, but this is where we need to strap on our work boots and really get after it.

All three of the cowboys had their own "Why." The first cowboy's *why* was to enjoy the moment and not worry about the future. The second cowboy's *why* was that he just wanted to do enough to be comfortable. And the third cowboy's_*why* was to eventually own everything. Each used a portion or all of their crayons (talents) to achieve this dream.

I have had a coaching career full of life-changing moments. One of these came when I had the great opportunity to assist Tim Weiss, assistant strength and conditioning coach, with training the University of Arkansas men's basketball team.

These were some of the hardest working individuals I've ever had the chance to be around. During one of the early workouts, I told the players that I had three questions for them. I told them that they didn't have to give me an answer that day but that I needed an answer as soon as they had it.

The three questions were:

1) Why did you come to the University of Arkansas to play basketball?

They didn't hesitate. It was unanimous; they all said they wanted to win the National Championship. There was a lot of chest bumping and posturing.

2) What are you willing to do to accomplish your dream?

Again, there was brave talk. Proclamations of jumping the highest building, swimming oceans, "lifting the house." I quieted the group again, and I finally asked them the third question.

3) Are you sure?

There was a moment of silence as they all looked around the group. Then Scotty Thurman said, "Bring it on. You can't make us quit on our dream."

We tried—not to make them quit on their dream, but to test their commitment and resolve. It is simple to speak grandly in the stillness of peace, but when you're in the heat of battle, are the speech makers willing to stand by their words? We had the athletes working hard every single day they were under our care. They were working on their flexibility, mobility, and stability. The great athletes we were working with became better athletes by the movement drills and prescribed weightlifting.

We couldn't make them back down off the answers they had given. When they got tired, Tim would ask them if they were done, and they would rally. Each of them finished that off-season pulling each other through the work they had. The head basketball coach, Nolan Richardson, was even more relentless with his "40 Minutes of Hell" basketball philosophy. Coach Richardson would run the opponents off the floor. Full-court press and fast-break basketball would break down their opponent by halftime. In order to accomplish this game plan, the basketball staff would work the players relentlessly with drills that forced them to be constantly on the move. The chaos they caused became normal to the players under Coach Richardson's tutelage. The off-season training plan complemented the head coach's style so well that the team went on to win the 1994 NCAA Men's Basketball National Championship.

I have since asked those three questions to every team I have ever coached. The answers are usually the same. Everyone wants to be the best. Everyone will do "anything" to accomplish their goals. But when the hammer hits the nail, when the rubber hits the road, this is where the difference comes. Those who are committed to the dream and the cost will endure whatever it takes to see it through.

This is the *Why*.

Why are you here? Why is this important to you? Why is it too important not to quit?

No Excuses

Too many people put qualifiers on their life. "I will work hard every day, except on the weekends because I need a break." To be successful, no qualifier can be added. If you want to be the best, you need to do everything as hard as you can—no excuses. If you are working with a team, you need to be pushed and be willing to push those who are not holding up their end of the bargain.

Champions live by the same motto, more or less: They are willing to work longer and harder than their opponents are willing or able. Notice I prefaced that by using the word "live." I have heard a lot of people say these words, and I understand why—it's a good sound bite.

But because most teams don't understand their *why*, they aren't able to hold up their end of the deal. In some locker rooms, you'll be able to find individuals who can live up to working hard every day… but inspiring the rest of the team to give up their weekends, to work late, to get in early, and to be totally committed just doesn't happen. When an entire team or company buys into this mindset—that they are willing to pay the price and sacrifice their current state of being because they know their motivation for doing so—that's when great things can happen.

Champions work longer and harder than their opponents are willing or able.

With all the teams I've coached, I've seen a similar scenario. Everyone answers the three questions on Monday with great enthusiasm, but on Tuesday, there is a drop-off in the teams who are not committed to their *why*. When I ask the leaders of these teams where their team members were, they jump headfirst into the "not my problem" syndrome. This syndrome allows parts of the team or group to decide when and to what degree they are willing to participate. This is the difference between a team finishing the season by winning a championship and those who finish the season making excuses. The truth is, success only comes when the entire group, team, business, or organization is on the same page.

The success in my professional career that came in 1978 at Mason City High School, in 1994 at Arkansas, in 1997 at Trinity Valley, 1998 at Tennessee, 2004 and 2005 at USC, and 2013 in Seattle only happened because every piece of the process was working together. No one was working outside his strengths or trying to be someone else, and no one was off doing his own thing. Everybody was working at his capacity to achieve the same goal—winning a championship.

Now, in Chapters 1 and 2, we've learned tough lessons, asked ourselves tough questions about who we are and who we want to be, and identified our strengths and talents. But I must warn you, Chapter 3 is quite possibly the most challenging part of this entire process. However, if you continue to put in the work and trust the process, I assure you that you'll be well on your way to a life of significance.

Chapter 3

The Deep End

<blockquote>A ship in harbor is safe, but that is not what ships are built for.
—John A. Shedd</blockquote>

When I was 8 years old, my parents put me in swim lessons at the local municipal swimming pool. I had no problem being in the water… as long as I could put my feet on the bottom of the pool. I moved through the swimming lesson progressions no problem—from Beginners I in my first year of swim lessons to Beginners II in my second year. Everything went *swimmingly*. Even Beginners III, in my third year of lessons, was going well! That was, until my swim group was informed of the test that would allow us to move into the Intermediate level of swim lessons.

We had to swim the width of the pool and back four times using the front crawl and backstroke. I could do that no problem—again, as long as my feet could get to the bottom of the pool. The major hitch was the second stage of the test. This entailed us having to jump off the low diving board and swim to the edge of the pool… in the deep end!

"Houston, we have a problem."

I knew I couldn't do that. I couldn't even *look* into the deep end. I once walked out to the end of the diving board on my own, and while looking down, I developed "aquatic vertigo." Alright, I have no idea if that's a real thing; I just know that as I stood at the end of the diving board, it looked like there was no bottom to the pool, and the world as I knew as it began to spin. The lifeguard yelled to me to either jump in or get off the board. I opted for the latter. From that day on, I knew I would never be able to jump into the bottomless pit.

Testing day came, and I took my spot in my normal swimming area—on the shallow side of the rope that denoted the depth change in the water. My swim instructor walked over and said, "Chris, you need to be on this side of the rope to complete your test."

You see, the major problem here was that the rope was what divided the shallow end of the pool from the deeper end.

"But I've swum on this side of the rope the whole summer!" I whined.

"Well, your test won't count if you don't swim with the rest of the class."

I shrugged my shoulders and headed toward the middle of the pool. The instructor probably thought she had talked me into endangering my life. Instead of joining the class, I continued walking toward the fence, picked up my towel and my Sears Winner tennis shoes, and walked over to the fence where my mom was standing.

"What's the matter?" she asked.

"I'm done. I can't do it."

"Chris, you will get back out there, and you will do the test."

"The only way that's going to happen is if the pool freezes over or Moses shows up to separate the water," I said, my arms crossed against my chest.

Since neither was going to happen, I walked out of the swim facility and sat on the hood of our family station wagon. My mom eventually joined me, and we got into the car.

"I hope you are happy with yourself. You'll be the laughingstock of your class, Chris."

I shrugged and said, "But I'll live to tell my side of the story."

Mom cut her eyes at me as she backed the station wagon out of the parking spot. "Just wait until your dad hears about this one."

Yes, I was ridiculed by my brothers and endured the sideways looks from my mom and the look of disgust from my father, but I didn't drown. I won the day.

The next year, I knew the rules. I psyched myself up by swimming on the other side of the rope. Though the pool dropped off quickly, I was able to use the rope to hold myself up when I started to sink.

When test day came around again, the instructor took pity on me and let me swim in my new normal spot—mostly because I was *technically* not in the shallow end. Thankfully, I accomplished the swim portion of the test. Then, together as a class, we walked to the diving board. Student after student jumped in, some with nice dives, some cannonballs, some pencils, and several belly flops. I had a great time cheering and jeering my swim classmates. The instructor turned to me and said with a smile, "OK, Chris, you're the last one."

I looked at her, then at the diving board, and finally at the blue darkness at the bottom of the pool. I shrugged my shoulders, walked to the ladder leading up onto the diving board, picked up my towel and my Sears Winners, and headed to the fence.

I found my mom at the fence watching my sister, who had just passed her test with Beginners I. Mom asked if I swam, to which I replied, "Yes, I did!" She was all smiles… until the swim instructor walked up and informed me (and my mom) that if I didn't jump into the deep end and swim to the edge, I would fail Beginners III… *again*. I looked at her for a second while finalizing my decision. Without saying a word, I headed out through the locker room to sit on the hood of the family station wagon, waiting for my sister to finish.

Once again, I was ridiculed by my brothers, and as soon as she finished and walked up, my sister joined in on the fun. My mom looked at me with pity, and my dad looked at me with disappointment.

However, I knew I could weather the verbal beating because I had survived another near-death encounter.

Fast forward 365 days. It was testing time for the Beginners III swim class. I swam like Mark Spitz—the guy who won 7 gold medals in the 1972 Olympics—in the swim part. Then we marched over to the diving platform. After the whole class had finished their various "dives," it was my time to shine. I walked to the edge of the diving board, looked into the abyss, and promptly turned around. Can you guess what came next?

You better believe I climbed down the ladder, picked up my towel and my Sears Winners, and headed to the station wagon.

I never did pass Beginners III. My parents pulled me out of swim lessons the next summer because my little sister had caught up to me, and my parents didn't want to embarrass me. I'm not sure if they didn't want *me* to be embarrassed or if they were actually concerned about *their* embarrassment. I could hear the possible conversation.

> Friendly Parent: "Hey, do you have any kids in swim lessons?"
> Mom: "Yes, I have two."
> Friendly Parent: "Where are they?"
> Mom: "The blonde-headed girl swimming like a fish and the big-headed boy walking in the shallow end."
> Friendly Parent: "Big for his age?"
> Mom: "No, just sucks as a swimmer."

So, what's my point here? It's simple. I did not trust the swim instructor, who swam in the Olympic qualifiers, standing at the end of the diving board. I did not trust the two lifeguards, who were collegiate swimming all-Americans working at the pool during the summer, who were on hand watching each swim student as they individually jumped into the diving well. I did not trust Mr. Coville, who ran the pool in the summer and coached the high school swim team to multiple state championships.

But worst of all, I didn't trust myself.

What would have happened had I jumped into the pool? I would have hit the water. I would have stopped sinking—eventually. I would have floated to the top. I would have paddled to the edge and got out. But I could not accept this reality at my age. The fear was bigger than the truth. I allowed the worst possible scenario—the one I made up in my mind—to block my path.

Here is the sad truth: There are adults in this world who have done the same thing in their professional lives. They have sold themselves a false bill of goods. They have given their fears power. So much power, in fact, that they became stuck in the job they were so comfortable doing.

One day, they stood on the edge of moving to the next step in their climb up the ladder. However, it seemed like there would be no safe place to land if their step did not work out. Instead of trusting themselves, they moved back to the other side of the rope and stayed where they were safe, where they could always touch the bottom of the pool.

As promotions and opportunities came to them, they never were interested. They became the best at what they were doing, but in the end, they were afraid to tempt fate. This chasm that they had built in their minds prevented them from moving onward and upward with their professional lives.

Even though there were safety nets all around them—people who were on their side and wanted them to succeed, who were there to help assure them that their "risky" step was not professionally fatal as they had been telling themselves.

I would have never been an Olympic swimmer, but had I conquered that fear, what could I have accomplished? I'll never know because I played it safe. What about people fearing to push forward in their profession? They may never take that next step up the corporate ladder. They may let a job pass by that was actually made for them. Remember, good jobs usually don't open up; rather, you make them good jobs through your hard work.

> **Good jobs usually don't open up; rather, you make them good jobs through your hard work.**

Maybe they would have found their niche. Maybe this step would have led them to the next and then the next and then the next. But they will never know because they didn't trust themselves or the people around them.

Doubting Our Destiny

Doubting ourselves is not a unique occurrence. When Michelangelo was commissioned to paint the Sistine Chapel, he turned it down because he was a sculptor, not a painter. But the pope saw in Michelangelo what he didn't see in himself. He saw that Michelangelo was only working a small percent of what he had inside him.

Abraham Lincoln was constantly filled with doubt as he pushed our country through one of the hardest periods a president has had to preside over. Julius Caesar visited the statue of Alexander the Great when he was 30 years old and felt his life had no value as he realized that by the time Alexander was 30, he had conquered the known world.

Thomas Edison was sent home from school after only three months because his teacher felt that he was intellectually disabled. Track and field gold medalist sprinter Wilma Rudolph was stricken with polio and never thought she would walk again without leg braces. As a youngster, Mahatma Gandhi was a timid, shy boy who was afraid of the dark. Mary Anne Evans, better known by her male pen name George Eliot, doubted herself so far as to use a man's name instead of her own.

The point I'm beating to death here is that we all have doubt. Even the most confident will have their moments. And it is OK to have doubts! But we need to find our way around the walls that we ourselves build to hide behind.

The German philosopher/author Johann von Goethe urges us to, "Just trust yourself, then you will know how to live." But that's the problem. We have put ourselves in this situation. If it were as simple as "just do it," there would be no need for self-help books or motivational speakers.

I went from a kid who was afraid to jump into a city swimming pool surrounded by lifeguards to standing, by myself, in front of hundreds of the most powerful people in business and sports. Here are the three principles that

have helped me to gain confidence in myself and break down the walls of unbelief. I've dubbed these as the three keys to trust:

1) Understand yourself

2) Surround yourself with people you trust

3) Earn the trust of others

Let's take a look at each of these three points as we learn how to swim in the deep end together.

Key #1: Understand Yourself

I have actually already spoken at length about the first step in a previous chapter—understanding yourself. However, I'd like to take this knowledge a step further.

When I understand my strengths and weaknesses, I know what I can do and can't do. I know I am a motivator and a great leader in the area I know best. At one time, I thought it was on the football field. However, I quickly came to understand that I was not cut out to be a football coach. I didn't have the little intrinsic things that make a good coach great. My biggest issue on the football field was thinking two or three steps ahead while juggling the clock, personnel, and defensive adjustments. It's just not who I am. Instead of doing what I couldn't do, I found what I loved to do. I moved out of the football coaching profession into the strength coaching profession. I understand *this* area completely. I am a great fundamental teacher. I am a great motivator.

Most of all, I have a great mind in organization, helping me create a sound program that will develop athletes the coaching staff need to accomplish *their* goals.

I encourage you to take some time to go through the process of evaluating your strengths and weaknesses. You can go online and find a simple assessment test or do like I did: Take a piece of paper and draw a vertical line down the middle. Then list what it is that you do well, as well as the things you struggle with that might adversely affect your progress along your path to success. It may be a shot to your ego, but it will also free you from spreading yourself out too thin in your professional aspirations. When I removed the need to be a football coach from my professional ambitions, I was able to become a sharpshooter in my development and progression as a strength coach.

Strength	**Weakness**
Motivator	Play calling and sequencing
Short / Long-term planning	Adjusting to defensive changes
Teacher / Technical coach	Planning 2 or 3 plays ahead
Leader / Organizer	Game management decisions
Loyal	Need to be in the limelight

Everything I was good at fit perfectly with what I became—a strength coach, as well as what I am today, which is a motivational speaker / author. Everything I didn't do as well was what I needed to do to be a football coach.

It was hard on my ego to tell myself these things. But I had to face the truth, or I would have continued to spin off on a path that would not result in me living my best life. Now, this isn't a one-time assessment. I continue going through this process every few months to check my decisions along my professional path, and I encourage you to do the same.

Key #2: Surround Yourself with People You Trust

We are told that the notorious gangster Al Capone once said, "Be careful who you call your friends. I'd rather have four quarters than one hundred pennies." I only recently heard this quote but have lived out this principle for most of my life. I've never been one who "runs with the crowd." Though I have many people I regard as my friends, my "quarters" were the first of the dozens of calls I got when I won a Super Bowl, and they were the only calls I got when I lost the next one.

> Be careful who you call your friends. I'd rather have four quarters than one hundred pennies.
> —Al Capone

Your four quarters are the people in your inner circle. The people you trust the most in this world. It doesn't have to be four; it can be one or a dozen. It's totally up to you. However many you have, these are the people you trust with your deepest, darkest secrets because most of the time, they were there with you when they happened! They also know you better than anyone in the world. Most importantly, they should have two traits.

First, they have your best interest in mind when you ask them their opinion. Second, they aren't afraid to tell you the truth. Not "their truth," or a truth that is advantageous to them and maybe not so good for you. *The* truth and nothing but. The ability to accept the advice and warning from others is a great skill to learn. You may not like what you hear, and you don't have to follow it blindly, but it should make you pause and reflect on what you are about to do.

You know these are your quarters when you go against their advice, and they still have your back. Too many times, your "friends" will bail on you when you go out on your own. If that's the case, then they really weren't your quarters; they were simply acquaintances you picked up along your journey.

Of my four quarters, I am not nearly as smart as any of them and, by far, am the least talented. Additionally, none of them are in each other's social circle, nor do they live in the same state as any of the rest. Now, let me add a disclaimer: My wife, Louon, is my best friend, and we *do* live in the same state. In the same house, even. But I digress.

I think the only things I bring into friendship are being doggedly loyal, a consistency in telling the truth, and the desire to help the other person in any way that I can. I have high standards for what a friend is, and I live by these standards regarding my own friends.

Not only is trust in *yourself* vital, as we already learned, but your ability to surround yourself with people you trust is just as important. The chance of someone making a great change by themselves is not unheard of, but it *is* rare. Thomas Edison had all of his people at Menlo Park doing the groundwork to help him achieve his status. Alexander the Great ruled the "civilized world" during his reign, but he didn't do it alone. Vince Lombardi, Dr. Martin Luther King, Jr., Mother Teresa—none of them did it all on their own. They are the face of their achievements, but the truth is, they surrounded themselves with people they trusted.

So, how do we seek out our quarters? I think the emphasis is to truly vet these people to make sure they want what is best for you. No jealousy, no good-time friends (those who are there for the party but mysteriously go missing when it's time to clean up).

Here are the top three things that I look for when I am vetting a person in both my working and personal world.

1. How do they treat other people?

When you are with this person, do they gossip and talk about other people behind their backs? If so, you should be wondering what they say about you when you aren't around. Are they giving you helpful information, or are they trying to position themselves?

2. What are their professional or personal goals?

Do they profess to have all the "answers" but never use their knowledge to improve their position in life? Do they always have excuses for why they aren't in a leadership position since everyone they work with is an "idiot"? Are they satisfied with where they are, and do they want you to keep them company?

3. What do they bring to the table?

Does their background give them a basis for their advice? Do they motivate you to be better than they are? Are you always the one that starts the line of communication?

For now, let's talk about this in the context of the workplace.

First, if the person you are working with is constantly backstabbing and taking advantage of people around them, they won't hesitate to use the knife on you one day. These people are miserable to be around, constantly tearing others down.

They won't hesitate to put you down the first chance they get. Bad people don't see people differently. They are in this "game" of life for one thing: To use anyone they can to climb higher on the ladder, no matter what happens to those closest to them.

On the other hand, if they are kind and considerate, open doors for people, and are uplifting to those they come in contact with, they have passed the first hurdle. If they are quick to help someone they don't know, they will be even quicker at being there when one of their closest friends is in need.

Second, if someone is hoping to use you to climb up the ladder by taking credit for your hard work in a project, they are using you as a step—not trying to be your friend. They see you as someone they can manipulate to look better in the eyes of management. They want the position but are not willing to do the work to EARN the position.

A friend will help lift a person up but is not there to be carried. But when you find said person, who will be there when you need them, don't just contact them when you "need" something. This is selfish and one-sided. You don't want this kind of friend, so don't *become* this kind of friend.

When you look at their past, have they been consistent in their professional and personal pursuits? In other words, are they like a tornado, bringing destruction everywhere they go? These people bring chaos into every *life* they touch as well. They may have been fun to be around at one time in your life, but then you changed your focus and your goals. Now, this person is toxic to your professional growth. This type of person needs to be avoided at all costs. If you see one coming your way, run for cover.

Third, ask yourself the following question: What makes them worthy of your friendship? I know that might sound arrogant, but frankly, your friends should not be a random collection of unworthy characters. Think about it this way: If you had a child, who would you want them to hang out with? Thugs, drugs, and slugs, or ambitious people who want the best for your child and are willing to help them in any way possible?

What makes people worthy of your friendship?

This is how I have, through perspective, found the group of people that I have as my four quarters. For me, sometimes it wasn't as clear-cut as I have made it sound. But in the end, the relationships I had through my professional career that were toxic were eventually removed from my circle. Today, I do a much better job at "vetting" individuals. Experience has given me these guidelines, which I follow very closely.

My wife will get upset when one of her acquaintances shows their true colors. My response is, "That's OK; we know who they are now." And we move on. Just one less person we need to send a Christmas card to!

We Few, We Happy Few

Most of the time, your quarters are there in spirit. You don't need to talk to them daily. You know they're there, and, more importantly, they know *you* are there when they need you. That feeling when someone has your back in your worst times is a great one.

Throughout my coaching career, I have had the honor to go into games with some great *teams*. I emphasize the word "team" because I have also gone into a few games with a bunch of individuals. Each time every member was fighting for the same objective, that TEAM came out victorious. When individuals with their own agendas entered the playing field, the game didn't turn out as well.

A great example of playing as a team can be seen in Super Bowl XLVIII in New Jersey. The media had already given the victory to Peyton Manning and the Denver Broncos, but they did not count on our rabid Seahawk fans who had traveled across the country. The cheering was deafening as Peyton led his team onto the field for the first series. The fans got louder. The ball was snapped before the QB was ready—a disconnect between the center and the Hall of Fame quarterback showing their heartbeats were not in sync, or whatever you would prefer to call it. The ball flew past Peyton, and we earned a safety. The game was over. We were unbeatable that day because we played as one. There was something missing the whole day on the other sideline: trust. The Broncos might argue with that, but it was clear from my point of view on that day.

This type of trust doesn't just happen in a football game. It can happen in a meeting room, an office complex, or in your life. It is the trust that happens when all of your quarters, team, company, or family come together for that defining moment. It is the tipping point between success and failure. Winning or losing. Love or hate.

My favorite example of trust winning the day occurred in October of 1415. The King of England, Henry V, had been fighting his way through France trying to get to the coast and then back to England. Though there isn't an exact count, Henry had between 6,000 and 8,000 troops, and the French had between 14,000 and 15,000.

The outcome was based upon trust. At this time, the knights of the English army could have walked off the field of battle. The nobles would have been ransomed back to their families in England. The commoner would have been made into a prisoner or put to death.

If the commoner walked away, he would eventually have been captured and put to death or made a prisoner of France. If he was able to avoid capture and make it back to England, he would have been put to death for desertion. In the end, England might have fallen after the King was captured.

Both groups, the nobles and the commoners, fought with and for each other and England. William Shakespeare writes about this event in his play *Henry V*. In this play, Henry V gives his pre-battle pep talk. Granted, Shakespeare wasn't there for the battle, writing his play almost 185 years after the battle. But the St. Crispin's Day speech is epic.

We few, we happy few, we band of brothers;
For he today that sheds his blood with me
Shall be my brother
Be he ne'er so vile,
This day shall gentle his condition
And gentlemen, in England, now a bed
Shall think themselves accursed they were not here
And hold their manhood's cheap while any speaks
That fought with us upon St. Crispin's Day.
Henry V by Shakespeare
Act IV, Scene iii 53 - 67
Eve of the Battle of Agincourt 10 / 25 / 1415

Every time I read that, I get fired up. I know Henry himself didn't say that. But he was the underdog, fighting on foreign ground, and he won… BIG TIME! He must have said something that got everyone hyped up.

The English came together using the longbow and the battlefield conditions to win. It took great trust in each other to overcome such odds. This sentiment is echoed in Shakespeare's words, "We few, we happy, we band of brothers." I have been part of many contests, and several times we were the underdog who prevailed. The only way it happened was the trust that the team, the band of brothers, had for each other. People sacrificed their well-being to be there for their teammates. Each time we won a game as the underdogs, we would continue the run over the rest of the schedule.

Examples of trust adding confidence to your cause are easy to find in sports and in war, but what about life? What about *your* life? Have you ever come home with trepidation, only to have your confidence lifted by your family? This is the same feeling a team has when they are in the locker room before the game. Everyone is supportive, lifting each other up. This courage generated between teammates can lift each person to do what may seem impossible.

In this same way, your successes might have been impossible without the support of the person next to *you*. The person who is shouldering the same burden you are. The person that has pushed you to always be the best. The person that wants you to be successful.

This confidence is what turns losses into victories and a professional leap of faith into the turning point of a career, and we get it from trusting those who are closest to us—our four quarters. These are the people who put wind in our sails, allowing us to maximize our potential and continue along our path to significance.

Key #3: Cultivating Trust

Now that you are on the path to trusting yourself and surrounding yourself with people you can trust, you can finish the circle by working on how *you* can be trusted by those around you.

The bottom line is that you must cultivate the trust of those who work with you and/or for you, *and* you must gain the trust of the people you work for.

Let's say your goal is to accomplish a set number of objectives within a specific period of time. If you have the trust and support of the people you work with, you will be able to rally the troops to make it a group effort because they know they are part of a team. Then, those who work for you will feel that their work is valued and being put into action, and the people you are working for will see how you streamlined the operation and are hitting the numbers that they need to see a profit!

Building trust isn't that difficult, but it must be something you work at every single day. In my experience, I've found that there are three qualities that build trust. They are:

1) Communication

2) Consistency

3) Care

Let's take a look at each of these for a moment.

Communication: Earning Trust

When I was coaching, I had two rules.

1) Be Early

2) Communicate

Being early was about respect for the organization, their teammates, and themselves. However, the second rule was of utmost importance. Rule #2 could trump Rule #1. If an athlete communicated with me about an issue they encountered, we could work out a plan that was mutually beneficial. My ability to communicate with the athlete was the most important factor in my ability to implement and run my training philosophy.

Communication is the difference between having a connection with those you work with, those that work for you, and those who work above you. When we have communication, we have a willingness to become part of the bigger picture.

There are two components involved in communication. The first is the hardest. You must *listen,* and not just listen, but listen to understand, not just respond. The second part is making sure everyone is on the same page and understands what is happening and where the organization is going.

Now, this is completely backward from what most people think. Most people think communication is about talking. However, to be an elite leader, communication is about listening first, so that when you speak, you are giving educated information. Too many times, leaders will speak from what they "think," not from what is actually reality.

In my experience, the athletes knew I would listen to them, so they would not hesitate to come to me with their training issues. Because of this connection, I had very few problems working with the athletes that I dealt with every day. This pattern of communication can be replicated throughout the organization.

Consistency: Routine and Expectations

Whether I'm operating as a coach or as a motivational speaker, consistency is the key to my success, especially when dealing with people on a daily basis. As a coach, the players knew exactly what to expect from me. I treated each player, coach, and staff member as a unique individual. As a speaker, I perform consistently so that the client and the audience members receive a championship performance every time I step up to the podium.

This consistency is born out of two constants: routine and expectations.

As a strength coach, my daily routine was consistent each day the athletes met with me. The program varied every day, but the delivery was the same. I wanted to make the athlete as comfortable as possible and know who was showing up. I didn't let emotions sway me, nor did I deviate from the expected day's work. I even went so far as to dress the same every single day so that the athletes had a consistent picture when they walked into the facility. I cannot have athletes prepare to be the best if they aren't sure whom they are dealing with! When this issue is behind them, they can trust that they will be able to let *their* true selves come out to work every single day.

As a motivational speaker, my topic and stories change for each presentation. But the performance is consistent with what they had in mind when they asked me to come in to work with their groups or employees. I have found that consistency can be as simple as developing a daily routine or laying out what your expectations are.

When I am building trust with a new team or a new group of athletes, I want them to understand my expectations. During the first day—and for the rest of the training period—I continue to remind them that my expectations are no different than what their expectations should be: to be the best. If I do not perform to that level, then I have broken their trust. If they fail to meet my expectation, then I will continue to remind them of what it takes to go from good to great, great to elite, and elite to uncommon.

When I am on stage, I hold the audience's attention with movement and my voice, and I will make them think with my stories and lessons. I make sure I understand the vision of the client during pre-speaking interviews. During these meetings, I will come to an understanding of what is lacking in the corporation, organization, or the team, so that my message is consistent with the expectations of the individual who is bringing me in.

This all happens because of my meticulous planning and preparation. I leave nothing to chance because I don't get to press a reset. If I fail to perform up to my expectations, I will have lost that day. And because I only get one chance at every day, it is imperative that my routine is prepared to achieve the desired outcomes.

Caring: Employee / Employer

Caring is the final component of trust. Former President of the United States Theodore Roosevelt once said, "Nobody cares how much you know, until they know how much you care." I totally agree with this statement. I know when I felt that my work was appreciated, I didn't mind putting in the extra time to make sure that the work I was doing was the best possible that I could do.

Caring is a mindset that finds balance in the workplace. If an employee knows that management appreciates the job that is being done, they will care more about the work that they are doing. On the flip side, if there is a lack of appreciation, the work will suffer.

Whether you are in charge of a small group or of a large corporation, your attention to those who work "with" you should be of great importance. Did you catch that? I said the people who work WITH you. When you classify people as those who "work *for* you," it denotes that they are beneath you. How simple is it to change the terminology to those who work "*with* me"? A team of 10 always works better than 10 individuals who are subservient to an overseer.

> **Nobody cares how much you know, until they know how much you care.**
> **—Theodore Roosevelt**

Caring about an individual or group of people is simple.

Be specific. Don't give them a "you all have done a great job." To show that you actually care is to do your research about the process to get to the final product and attach names to the success of the job. If you have time to find the bad apples to remove them from the system, you have time to do the same work to find the great ones and give them the credit they earned.

Be mindful. If you are going to be quick to criticize, then you must all be quick to recognize in the same measure. You can't give too much credit for great work. If you want an action continued, then take consistent notice of the work. Don't wait for banquets to tell the people you work with that you appreciate their hard work.

Be present. Make sure you go into the work area and watch the work that is being done. Take time every day to be present. Ask questions, listen to responses, and make positive changes. These are the roots of communication.

Be real. Don't bring your personal photographer to capture your meeting with the common people. If you're on the production floor, don't bring an entourage. Loosen the tie, unbutton the jacket, and for the love, just don't wear the high heels. You're going to where the work is being done. They know who you are. You don't need the designer clothes.

If you are the one working for someone, you must also show them that you care about what you are doing by being the best employee you can be. Your value to the company is only that which you give back to the company. If you are doing only enough to just get along, they soon will be able to get along without you. Make sure you are an integral cog to the operation by simply caring more.

Be loyal. Don't talk your company down when you speak to others. If you don't like the work, find another job. Also, you may be speaking to someone who is in management, and your words may find their way upstairs.

Be early. Show the people around you that working is your priority. Being early is about respecting the organization and the people you are with, but most importantly, it is about respecting *yourself*. Being early (not just on time) means so much to you that you set your two alarm clocks. You set your clothes out so you're ready to go. When "life happens," your boss will be more understanding.

Be consistent. Always do your best work. Don't let the day of the week determine the quality of your work. If you strive for perfection in everything you do, your hard work will be noticed. If you struggle on Mondays and Fridays, then change your party schedule.

Be open. Do your best every day. If you are criticized, learn from the comments and grow. If you don't understand the critique, don't ask your work buddy. Go to the place where the criticism came from and ask them if they can elaborate on the issue. It may have been a "group criticism," and you are actually doing well. Or it may actually be an issue with your work. You can accept the criticism and change, or you can leave. However, I encourage you to be open to someone who is trying to make you better. If you are coming into a new work situation, be open to new ways of doing things. If you see areas that can be made more efficient, find a time to discuss it with your direct superior.

When there is caring on both sides of the ledger, a trust is formed. This trust comes from direct communication. When everyone is on the same page, great things will happen.

It All Comes Down to Trust

Trust is an essential ingredient to the success in both your personal and your work life.

We started the process by learning how to trust ourselves. If you don't trust the person you look at in the mirror every day, then why would anybody else trust you? So, we must learn to trust ourselves so that we can allow others to trust us.

To do this, we need to surround ourselves with people whom we can trust. Those who have our best interest in mind, who treat others like we want to be treated, and don't bring their own unwieldy baggage into our lives. Once this group is in place, we now have a group of people who can keep us moving along our path.

Once we trust ourselves and have our four quarters, we can then begin to get others to trust us. This is done in three areas. We must be great communicators, we must be consistent, and we must ultimately care about the well-being of those we depend on in our life and our work.

When we accomplish these stages of trust, we can accomplish some amazing things.

Chapter 4

Speak Your Truth

> If you want to
> make God laugh,
> tell Him about
> your plans.
> —Woody Allen

Woody Allen once said, "If you want to make God laugh, tell Him about your plans." Apparently, my mom kept God in stitches because she was the type of person who would load the wagon knowing she would find a team of horses to pull it.

Marian Catherine (Nieman) Carlisle passed away on October 19, 2018. Mom didn't graduate from college, yet she was the wisest person I have ever met. She was a teacher, a philosopher, a psychologist, a mediator, a chef, a grizzly bear with cubs, the best fan you would hope to have, and the last person in the world you would want to be mad at you. She was a domestic engineer—better known as a housewife. In her spare time, she was a master bridge player and a bingo wizard. Most of all, she was the greatest influence in my life. Her life was a lesson in grit and perseverance.

After Mom passed away, my wife, Louon, and I were going through old photo albums. We were collecting pictures of my family and me when I was younger. After going through several of the photo collections, I found a letter that was addressed to me but never sent.

I opened the letter, and it was like she was speaking to me from the other side. In the letter, she listed off 12 major life-changing events I had to work through to become who I am today. Mom wrote that in the lives of just about anyone else, any one of these events might have derailed them. But I found the strength and resiliency to overcome them *all*.

Things did not start well for me. I was born in 1962 with a physical deformity of my feet. The doctor consoled my mother, saying, "Except for the issue with his feet, he is a happy, healthy baby boy." He went on to tell her that I would never run like the other kids.

My mother's response?

"We'll see about that."

With constant foot and leg massages, orthopedic shoes, and all her love and support, I was soon chasing after my two older brothers, always trying to be part of their games. In the end, I never did run like the other kids. I ran *better* than them. In fact, I eventually ran well enough to earn a football scholarship at Chadron State College.

Being able to run and chase my brothers was a double-edged sword. On one hand, I was learning to overcome my physical handicap. On the other hand, I wasn't a skilled runner, and there were several times I fell because of this issue. Mom told me that about the time my front teeth had come in, I started to run. Because of my balance issues, it didn't take long to knock both of my brand-new teeth out. Because the premature loss of my teeth coincided with my learning to speak, I developed a speech impediment that started with slurring and then advanced into stuttering.

After several years of speech classes, the speech therapist called my mom in for a parent/teacher meeting. As they spoke in the speech room, I was able to listen because they had left the door slightly cracked. The speech therapist told my mom that though I was working hard, there wasn't much improvement. Because of the lack of change, she informed my mother that I would probably have this issue for the rest of my life. My mom listened politely.

In the end, the final comment that lit my mom's fuse was when the speech therapist said, "He will never be a public speaker." At that moment, my mom turned into a fierce protector. To the same tune by which she dismissed the doctor's comment about me not being able to run, she threw her a sharp "We'll see about that."

And with that, Mom picked up her jacket and purse and came through the door. I looked into the small room where the therapist sat, stunned. As my mom walked past me, I stood up and followed in her wake. My mom was a badass—a true mother grizzly bear. And since I was her cub, no one was going to give up on me.

My parents began working with me daily on my speech, correcting me when I needed it but always supporting me along my path. Many a time when I came into the house excited about something I needed to tell her, she would say, "Slow down and think about your words as you say them." This was a trick I still use today when I start a motivational talk. I start slowly until I get my rhythm. Throughout my childhood, it normally worked well. That is, until the day my brother Steve tried to burn down the garage in Boone, Iowa. I was trying to tell her what happened, and she hit me with the "slow down" coaching. Like I said, it was a good idea for me, but not so much for the garage.

Though I still need to remind myself to breathe and think about my words, today, my speech issues go by nearly undetected. While I was in college, I worked as a tour guide at Fort Robinson State Park during the summers, giving 15 to 20 tours a day, speaking to hundreds of people during each of my 8-hour shifts. In the coaching world, I have had the opportunity to speak in front of the team and the coaching staff and at pep rallies and awards banquets. As a motivational speaker, I entertain groups big and small each year, sharing about the lessons I have learned in my life and how they have carried me to accomplish all of my dreams.

I'd say my life proved that speech therapist wrong. And proved that my mom knew me better than anyone else ever would.

As I read through my mother's final letter to me, it was clear she saw my life as a test of perseverance. I could have stopped at any time to feel sorry for myself or to blame my current condition on my feet, my teeth, the car accident that nearly ended my life, the chicken house fan that nearly killed me, the cancer I beat to death, and the other incidents that I was taught to look at as merely an inconvenience.

So, why was it that I was able to move past those roadblocks life threw out in front of me while similar circumstances completely stop other people in their tracks? I believe it started with my mother speaking out her vision about what she *knew* she could make happen. When confronted with the words "He'll never run like other children" or "He'll never be a public speaker," she spoke the opposite as truth. She would not even let me think in any other way! She spoke out what *her vision* of the truth was going to be.

She "spoke" me into running. She "spoke" me into speaking without an impediment. She "spoke" me into accomplishing whatever I set my mind on doing. When I was diagnosed with cancer, and I told her that they had given me a 40% chance of surviving, she said, "We'll see about that." And here I am today, 20+ years since the doctors had nearly given up on me.

But my mom never did.

Use Your Gifts!

Because of my life experiences, I have to disagree with Woody Allen. I think God *smiles* when we tell Him our plans. He smiles because He is happy that we are taking the gifts that we are given and moving along our path to accomplish what we have been tasked to do in our lives. He may laugh, but not in a mocking way. Instead, I believe He'd be laughing because of how long it takes some of us to figure out something so simple: That we are strong enough to accomplish anything that we put our minds to.

I believe that when we pray to God (or whomever you might pray to), and we tell Him that we quit, that we give up, that we're just going to stop trying, He cries. We are all born with the gift of free will and a combination of talents (crayons, remember?) that **no one else in the world** is given. To waste these gifts is unforgivable, at least in my mind!

If you gave your children every gift they wanted for their birthdays, and they just sat on the shelf unused, how would you feel? I would be saddened. When we take all the gifts we are born with and don't use them to be the best we possibly can be, how does the Great Creator feel?

When we announce to the world that we are going to use our talents to accomplish the life we have been gifted, we are not taunting God; we are letting it be known that we are moving forward with the plan that has been made for us.

When we announce our plan, we are putting a stake in the ground. This is our starting point. And from here, we announce we are going to move farther down our chosen path.

By putting that stake in the ground, we also are asking to be held accountable by our closest friends—our four quarters. If we announce it on social media, we are letting the *world* know our intentions. No matter how you share intentions—whether you shout them from the rooftops or you whisper them to a close friend—you are asking people to hold you accountable. If you don't accomplish said plans, there will be people who are glad to hold your bold proclamations over your head. If you don't work well under pressure, then limit your exposure. But in any case, let *someone* know. Make sure this person, or group of people, are those who will motivate and lift you up so you can move forward with your goals.

Sharing my intentions out loud has proven to work for me and my career. I once told Nate Low when I was 10 years old that I would win a Super Bowl. I also refused to believe the nurse who told me that I would lose my hair and not be able to work as she slid the needle into my arm for my first chemo treatment. I followed my mom's lead and said, "We'll see about that." I never did lose my hair, and I never missed a day of work.

Now, I'm not the only one who has done this sort of thing. Let me give you some proof for why I believe so deeply in the phenomenon of speaking your dreams into reality.

A King Ain't Satisfied

On the first track on Bruce Springsteen's fourth album, *Darkness on the Edge of Town*, he tells us about his plans. "Badlands" is four minutes and three seconds of telling you what he wants and how he is going to get it. The part that has defined my life and is, in part, the impetus of this book, comes 1 minute and 35 seconds into the song. Springsteen tells us, "Poor man wanna be rich, rich man wanna be king. And a king ain't satisfied till he rules everything."

Springsteen puts it all out there. He won't be satisfied until he ascends to the highest point in the music business. In the song, he tells us that it isn't going to be easy, and too many of us "spend [our lives] waiting for a moment that just don't come." Instead of waiting for that "moment," a miracle, or your lotto number to come up, we need to work for those goals.

> Too many of us spend our lives waiting for a moment that just don't come.
> —Bruce Springsteen

"Workin' in the fields till you get your back burned. Workin' 'neath the wheel till you get your facts learned."

We need to persevere through the hard times and not give up. We need to understand *why* we are doing what we are doing and make sure that the movement, no matter how slow, is in the direction that will take us to our destination.

The pace is secondary to the end goal. Ralph Waldo Emerson supposedly said, "Life is a journey, not a destination." In the chorus of "Badlands," Springsteen speaks to this point when he sings, "Keep pushin' till it's understood. And these badlands start treating us good."

What can we learn here? We've gotta keep moving. Don't get stuck in one place. Do the work that you need to do to get to where you want to be. This is best done by having short-term goals you can reach on your way to your dreams. Even when the dream seems far away, you can continue to make progress by accomplishing your short-term goals. When you have these goals in sight, you will stay motivated on the long road toward seeing your dream fulfilled and living a life of significance.

It is important to see that Springsteen puts his dreams into words, sings them as loud as he can, and then goes out and makes them come true. He went from a self-proclaimed hippie to a 70-year-old rock-and-roll icon who will still fill huge arenas and put his heart and soul into every performance for three hours—without a break or an opening band!

This is precisely where he is different than most people; he not only told us what he was going to do, but he worked hard (and likely struggled immensely) to make it come true. He played every small venue, shopping center opening, high school dance, and small club that he could to make it big. He changed his band members, his style, and how he went about writing his songs. He battled to get playtime on major radio stations. He even went to war against his own management. In the end, he owns and controls all aspects of his music.

In other words, "He rules everything."

The reason this song strikes a chord with me is that I started my professional career in a small high school with aspirations of coaching at the highest levels of the sport. I moved from opportunity to opportunity, each step putting me closer to accomplishing my dreams.

I climbed the professional ladder from a high school coach (poor man), to the junior college and college level (rich man), and finally to the NFL and into motivational speaking (king). It took great effort, energy, and commitment to move through the stages, but I could not have done it without having *announced* my plan.

If I hadn't proclaimed my intentions to continue to advance through each level of my professional career, I would have only been held accountable for obtaining my dream by me. And that is a *lonely* path. When you're only accountable to yourself, it's too easy to give yourself a break. When I announced my path to those around me, I opened the door to criticism. But because I have always thrived when doubted, I excelled beyond most people's wildest dreams of what I could accomplish.

Putting my dreams into words forced me to deal with the reality of them. It made me listen to how crazy it all sounded as I watched the people I was telling. If my words were met with uncontrollable laughter, I needed to assess whom I was speaking with, as maybe they were the wrong audience. Or maybe I was talking "crazy talk," but who really knows. I found these moments of self-reflection occur when I am writing just to write. If what I write doesn't sound like "me," I can reel in the thought process and check in about why it doesn't flow. Most of the time, I find that I was writing about someone that I am not. My "bullshit alarm" is highly sensitive because I know myself.

Now, I need you to know that speaking my dreams into existence started small. I just told my closest friends. I have spoken about writing a book for a long, long time. And now I am finally doing it! I've started and stopped several runs at accomplishing this dream. The problem was that I didn't have enough answers, or maybe I still had too many questions. But this close circle of friends kept moving me down the line.

I didn't start by speaking out my dream to a larger audience. I would be a little leery of putting it on the Internet. With today's landscape, I would really hesitate to open myself up to the ridicule of those who hide behind their screens, likely never accomplishing a thing in their lives. I'd encourage you to gain a resume before you open yourself up to the faceless masses.

I started with my four quarters and then expanded to associates in my profession. I then had the opportunity to expand my circle to include the football teams I have worked with. What a great atmosphere it was, surrounding myself with a group of people who would not hesitate to call "bullshit" on my crazy talk. When I was given a chance to speak out my dreams in team meetings before games, it was really special. This gave me the strength to share with larger and larger groups.

Though I now speak to groups about how to maximize their potential, I still continue to talk about my next "move." I share about not only how I got to where I am but how I plan on moving to the greatest extent in the profession. It wouldn't be fair for me to stand in front of them and tell an audience to speak their dreams into reality if I wasn't willing to do it myself!

I have found the farther I have pushed along my path that there are fewer naysayers because I have accomplished all that I have spoken about in the past. Now the questions sound like this:

"When will you get it done?"

"How are you going to make it happen?"

In the backyard of my youth, recreating the NFL plays of the week, I was already talking about what I would accomplish when I was old enough to play organized football. When I was playing on the football field of my teens, I was talking about what I would do when I was playing in college. While I was on the field and moved up to coaching on the sidelines, I was talking about how I was going to coach my own teams one day. While coaching college football, I started to speak of coaching in the NFL. Now, I went from speaking at clinics and rotary meetings to speaking to bankers, realtors, sports teams, and the largest corporations in this country.

Throughout this journey of speaking out my dreams, it was as if I were going on a trip. I told people where I was and where I was going to end up. Each stop along the way was needed to fill my proverbial tank. In the end, I am where I had set my course to be, and it is only because I was able to speak my dreams to people who held me accountable as I moved down the line.

Putting Dreams into Action

In 1871, a fire ignited in the heart of downtown Chicago, Illinois. It was so massive that it wasn't just the "Chicago Fire"; it was the *Great Chicago Fire*—not to get mixed up with any lesser fires that burnt parts of the city. At the time, most of the buildings in Chicago were built with wood framing, so the fire gutted the young city. After the fire, several business leaders got together to see if anybody was planning to stay in the burned-out city. Many of them said they were done. They had already lost everything, so they were going to move on. In their minds, it would simply take too long to get the city back to where it once was.

We'll see about that.

One of these businessmen, Marshall Field, stepped up and said, "On this spot, I will build the greatest store in the world." And he did. Marshall Field's department store became the largest of its time.

Marshall Field not only announced his plan, but he doubled down when he said he would build the *largest* store. He could have put up a small shop, and he still would have built a store on the spot he said he would. But that wasn't good enough for him. He was going to build a gigantic shopping space in the midst of smoldering buildings. He had several naysayers, but he simply used their negativity as fuel to push him further down the line.

In 1992, I became the head football coach at Subiaco Academy. My first meeting with the alumni came during the summer after I had been hired. I still remember it today. After being introduced to the audience, I began a fire and brimstone talk about my coaching philosophy. I told the assembled alumni my plans: "I will develop a football team that you will be proud of. One that will be better trained, both mentally and physically, than they have been in the past.

"In order to do this, I will currycomb the current student body for any individual who wants to be part of something special." I had their attention. The team's numbers were down to the 30 players, and much of the student body had felt excluded.

I then spoke out my dream. "This change will not come overnight, but over the next few years. This metamorphosis will only come through hard work. But we will do this work together. The individual players will become a team."

They were on the edge of their seats. "The genesis of this turnaround will occur in the physical development of the athletes in the weight room."

Now, remember, the weight room was a dingy, dirty area housed in the basement of the fieldhouse on campus. The equipment consisted of two rickety bench presses, two square tubed squat racks, and an assortment of rusty mismatched weights.

When I mentioned that the beginning of the changes would take place in the weight room, one of the alumni called out, "You better get the boys their tetanus shots before you start!"

This is where I changed my speaking tone. "That is true. The weight room is an embarrassment and a joke—much like this team has been."

This made the group sober up. "If you dream of this team becoming something special, what are you going to do to help it become what we all dream of? How will you make a difference? If you can't score any more touchdowns, how are you going to leave your mark on this team?"

And they came through.

The men of Subiaco Academy put forth several thousand dollars to get the transformation started. After four years, the weight room had four Olympic platforms, four standard bench presses, four solid squat racks, two leg presses, thousands of pounds of top-quality weights, bumper plates, and bars. The room had a rubber floor, record boards, and a fresh coat of paint. And most of all, we had a team that the alumni could be proud of.

This couldn't have happened had I not spoken my dream out loud. It wouldn't have happened had the alumni not heard the dream and committed themselves to make it come true. In the end, the dream still lives on for all of the sports at Subiaco Academy.

Lead by Example

In his inaugural address after winning the 1960 presidential election, John F. Kennedy stated, "Before this decade is out, we will land a man on the moon and return him safely to the earth."

Instead of one man, *three* men were sent, and on July 20, 1969, the lunar landing module of Apollo 11 landed on the moon, and Neil Armstrong and Buzz Aldrin went for a walk. And on July 24, all three men splashed down safely in the Pacific Ocean.

Kennedy didn't live to see the historic event occur, but he was the one who put the mission into words. As we've seen in the other examples in this chapter, sometimes speaking the dream out loud is the most important part of the process. Putting your dreams into words not only adjusts *your* thinking to a new possibility that may not have been imagined before but adjusts the perspective of everyone around you as well.

When I first came to the University of Southern California, I spoke to the head football coach, Pete Carroll, about what I could bring to the football team. I spoke out my dreams. I told Pete that I would help develop players into some of the finest athletes that would ever play college football. I told him about my philosophy of movement rather than focusing on raw strength alone, as other teams were doing. I spoke about instilling discipline in the athletes through consistency. And I said I would use every crayon in my box to motivate the athletes to the highest levels of the game.

In short, the philosophy was something like this: We would *prepare* at the highest level so that they could *practice* at the highest level, so in the end, they could *play* at the highest level.

After a developmental year (where we still went to a bowl game), we took off. In the nine years I was at USC, we were in nine bowl games. We won the conference championship seven times in a row. We were involved in three national championship-deciding games, winning two of them. We had three Heisman Trophy winners, and I was named strength coach of the year. The athletes we worked with set the bar for what football players could be if they worked hard and trusted the plan.

I am not saying I was solely responsible for the success of the teams that we had; I am only saying that I held up *my part* of the bargain. The coaches still coached, and the recruiters recruited hard-working young men whose character and work ethic melded with what was being taught within the program. And the whole thing worked like a Swiss watch.

Are You Willing?

The king of speaking success into reality, in my opinion, is Muhammad Ali. Ali is considered by some to be the greatest boxer ever to have put on a pair of boxing gloves. And what set him apart? Speaking out his dreams.

"I am the greatest, I said that even before I knew I was," he shared,, giving away part of his secret formula. Ali was a Golden Gloves champion as a young boy. In 1960, Ali (born as Cassius Clay) earned the Olympic gold medal in the Rome Olympics. In 1964, he defeated Sonny Liston to become the World Heavyweight Champion.

Many of Ali's fights are rated as the greatest fights of all time. Moreover, these were also during one of boxing's golden eras, when some of the most iconic boxers of all time were fighting. There were very few "easy" matches for the champ. Ali defeated, defended, and recaptured his crown over and over again against some of the all-time greats.

> **I am the greatest, I said that even before I knew I was.**
> **—Muhammad Ali**

Ali was never one to shy away from a microphone. His confidence in himself and his abilities was one of his greatest assets. Predicting the round that he would knock out his opponent became his hallmark. He spoke out his dreams and then went out and earned the respect that he deserved.

The first time I sat down with Russell Wilson, I could literally *feel* his confidence. This 5' 11", solidly built individual was brimming with enthusiasm. After two minutes of talking with him, he said, "Coach C, I'm going to be the starting quarterback this season."

"I don't have a dog in the hunt, so I will work all the quarterbacks to the same end," I replied.

He smiled and said, "I like that. All I need is a chance."

Knowing the staff, I knew he would get his opportunities. After the first rookie practice, I became a believer in his dreams. The kid could spin a ball. When the veterans came in for Organized Team Activities (OTAs), Russell was always early, eager to learn, and most importantly, he was willing to work.

In the first workout with the quarterbacks, I had an option on the leg strengthening portion of the workout. The athlete could choose to do leg presses or a back squat. Both are good exercises, but the leg press is less demanding, thus it does not bring the benefits that squatting does. The two veterans chose the leg press, while the young lion chose the back squat. This set his position in my mind. Russ understood that the easier of the two paths wouldn't help him accomplish his goals. He also understood that his legs were the primary driver for the velocity on the ball. Because of his choices, he would soon pass his competition. After the pre-season games, Russell became the starting QB.

After his first season, we sat down again. This time he boldly proclaimed that he would help take the team to a Super Bowl. And he did that, too. Well, actually, he helped us get to *two* Super Bowls (back-to-back). Russell does not lack in confidence, nor does he lack in the work ethic to actually *accomplish* his goals. I found the proclamations of his intentions refreshing. When Russ told me what he was going to do, I always knew it would happen.

All of the examples I just gave—Springsteen, Field, Kennedy, Ali, and Wilson—spoke out their dreams and then made them a reality.

Now, I can already feel what you're thinking. *All I have to do is say my dreams out loud, and they will come true? Are you crazy?*

Remember the old saying, "If something sounds too good to be true, it probably is"? Well, this is one of those times. Each of these men also had something else going for them. They were willing to put in the work and grind through whatever was in their way. And they were able to persevere through the hard times and setbacks.

To announce your intentions is a big step toward accomplishing your goals. Putting in the work to get there, however, is what sets the "kings" apart from the "poor men." The other musicians were not willing to play the small venues. The other businessmen did not put their money and effort into their plans. The other politicians were unwilling to do the dirty work and earn the support of their constituents. The other athletes *thought* that being great was a good idea but never gave it everything they had.

All of those people you view as successful all have one thing in common: They earned their success.

So, let's go to work.

Grind

Pain is inevitable.
Suffering is optional.
—The Dalai Lama

Grind

*1) To reduce to powder or small fragments
by friction.
2) To weaken or destroy gradually.*

(Merriam-Webster Dictionary)

Grind. It's a term a lot of people use. Unfortunately, it is all too often used in a negative light. Doing the foundational work is a "grind." Coming to work early is a "grind." Having to do the clean-up part of the job is a "grind." Working long hours to accomplish your goals is a "grind."

Often, simply doing the work that is part of the job is seen as "grinding."

However, if you ask me, I see the "grind" in a positive light. To me, I imagine the work I am doing as grinding up issues and using them as the foundation for me to build something great upon. I know the harder I go about my work—the harder I grind—the better things will turn out. Nothing good has ever happened to me that came easy. Working my way up the ladder allowed me to learn the nuances that helped me to develop athletes that win on *and* off the field.

I'll be honest; writing this book was a grind. But I loved every single step of the process. I had to do things that I once took for granted. For example, I used to be able to write for hours. I once spent an entire vacation "writing" in my notebook. Naturally, I thought that writing a book was going to be a breeze because I loved to write. However, it turned into a grind because I had to come face to face with a huge issue: who I was, who I am, and who I will become as a writer. Then, I reduced these issues into concrete answers through the use of words, while making sure the stories I told continued to connect with the reason *why* I was writing the book. As the process came to an end, I could (and still can) confidently say that I have never enjoyed a process more than writing this book.

The grind is nothing but hard work. To some, these are dirty words, but to others, hard work is an invitation to success. The difference comes in the attitude in which you go about your work. It's a "get to" vs. a "got to" proposition. If you don't enjoy your work because you never see the fruits of your labor, you will see hard work as something you've *got to* do. On the other hand, if you see hard work as a positive because you *get* to make a difference today, you will attack it with great enthusiasm, and it becomes a *get to*. You will only accomplish to the degree you are willing to work.

____

It's a "get to" vs. a "got to" proposition.

____

Don't get me wrong; if you have a job you love and feel as if you've never "worked" a day of your life, then it sounds like you are on track to an amazing life. But the bottom line here is this: If you don't like to work hard because working hard is hard work, then you better dial down your dreams.

At the core, leading a life of significance is all about the way you go about your daily grind… and the way you go about making your daily grind a positive is to follow your passion. If you're passionate about what you do, your grind becomes less about the labor and more about the results. If you can't wait to get your day started, the grind of waking up early goes away. If you love the small jobs that make up the pursuit of your passion, you will never be overwhelmed. When finishing up their work at the end of the day, some dread the process of cleaning up. However, when you see it as preparing your workspace for the next day, it becomes a labor of *love*.

You can only control what you can control, and your attitude is the one thing you get to control.

When I was growing up, I didn't see the need to mow the lawn at our house. But when I got older and bought my first house, I took pride in taking care of my lawn. The job was the same. The thing that was different was my *perspective*.

At the beginning of my coaching career, I was blessed to be around some great teachers. Ken Ippenson and Johnny Church kept their equipment rooms in pristine condition so they could put their hands on whatever it was they were looking for in no time. So, when I took over my own teams, I tried hard to make sure that my storage rooms were always in orderly condition.

Organizing my weight rooms was the same way. John Stucky, my mentor from the University of Arkansas and the University of Tennessee, demanded that all of the bars and machines were in line, the rods on the machines oiled, and the pads cleaned throughout the day. He said, "You never know when an all-American will walk in, and the weight room will persuade him to come to our school."

So, I made it a practice that before the weight room was closed down, the last coach there would make sure all the bars and weights were right and the doors were locked. Not only did we have the place ready for that elusive all-American who was a weight room clean freak, but it also promoted safety by reducing the number of potential items to trip on while walking through in the dark. When the lights went on and the athletes were working, they always knew where the implement or bar they needed would be.

Doing things right wasn't a chore; it prepared me to be better at what I was doing. Order shows control, while chaos shows confusion. When you start with order on the first day, it is easy to control the appearance and effectiveness of your home or workplace.

With the advantage of perspective in my pocket, I can look back now and pick out the most important parts of my experiences that allowed me to find the positive side of the grind. I have found five areas that kept me balanced through my 35 years of coaching and teaching, I call them the Five Ps.

They are:

1) Passion

2) Prepare

3) Practice

4) Perform

5) Persevere

Step One: Passion

"There is nothing outside of yourself that can ever enable you to get better, stronger, richer, quicker, or smarter. Everything is within. Everything exists. Seek nothing outside of yourself."
—Miyamoto Musashi

Passion about what you do and how you do it is critical to making sure you will never see your "grind" as a negative. When you are doing something or working toward doing something you truly love, it feels as if there is no clock or calendar, no job too big or small. This comes back to the need to understand who you truly are so that you can be doing what you are meant to do! When you understand "you," a course can be set, and you begin to move towards accomplishing the things that will allow you to find balance and flow. From balance and flow, you find harmony.

My passion is in the desire to help people down their paths so that they can achieve what they desire. My vehicles have been as a teacher, a coach, and now, as a motivational speaker. When I started my professional life, I thought that my passion came from winning championships, but I soon came to understand that winning and losing was secondary to the way that I was able to help my athletes accomplish their dreams and lead a life of significance. The icing on the cake was that as I helped others down their path, success followed!

Step Two: Prepare

> "A warrior is responsible for his weapons just as a master craftsman is responsible for his tools."
> —Miyamoto Musashi

In life, preparation is the beginning of all successful ventures. The way you prepare will determine how you finish. If you start sloppily, it will only go downhill from there.

Preparation is the foundation for anything you do. However, this is the problem: Most people see the planning and development stages as tedious because there are very few immediate returns. If you don't take the time to plan and work towards the future, small issues can become major problems. For instance, if you are in the construction profession and you don't order a crane before you need it, there may not be one around when it comes time to start your work, and you'll be behind schedule… which could cost you a job!

As a strength and conditioning coach, my life was all about preparation. At the NCAA collegiate level, I had 20 weeks (8 weeks in the spring, 4 weeks of spring football, and 8 weeks in the summer) to get my athletes to a place where they could compete with the best players in college football. My training philosophy was based on movement: The ability of an athlete to move allowed him to practice and perform at the highest level. I did not teach them the X's and O's of football; that was up to the football coaches. My job was to prepare them to do what the coaches needed them to do—faster, stronger, and with greater power and explosiveness.

I loved every minute I was with these athletes, helping them get better so they could go out and accomplish *their* dreams. Now, I put the same amount of time and energy into preparation as a motivational speaker. It just looks a little different.

Step Three: Practice

> "You must practice at the intensity of real life, or it becomes a game,
> which will soon lead to your defeat."
> —Miyamoto Musashi

Pete Carroll says that "Practice is everything." I agree with him. Well, I agreed with this fact even before I met him!

I've observed the top coaches in the world prepare championship teams—Barry Alvarez, Nolan Richardson, Scotty Conley, Pat Summitt, Phillip Fulmer, Vince Anderson, Pete Carroll, and Kris Richard—during the months, weeks and days leading up to the final game of the season.

Each of these coaches saw that their success in games was directly tied to their practice. They found that if their practices didn't mimic the tempo and the energy of the game, they would lose. When the intensity of practice wanes, there are breakdowns in fundamentals. When fundamentals fail, the structure of the team erodes.

Contrary to popular belief, practicing your craft is not a mundane or "boring" part of the grind. Practice allows you to make sure that everything you need to have happen will happen. I'm talking about people like Kam Chancellor, former NFL safety, hustling to knock the ball out of a receiver's hand as he reaches for the goal line. That didn't just happen. Every day, Kam *practiced* stripping footballs from the receivers' hands. When it happened in the game, it was a "great play," but it only happened because he worked on the fundamental skills in practice.

Now, let's take this off the playing field. I'm talking about having all of your slides ready for a presentation. Maybe you have a job interview coming up. Have you had a friend, your partner, or a colleague give you a practice interview? This could be the one thing that puts you in the front of the pack and not looked at as just another resume. Success doesn't just magically happen. It takes hard work. But in the end, the time you spend perfecting the little things pays off in giving you the chance to continue chasing your dreams.

If you are nervous about doing something, you need to practice doing it. When I am preparing to do a performance using magic, I will use mirrors and videotaping to make sure I don't give anything away. This is a regular practice for all magicians. Ballet artists will have danced their part of a performance for years before putting it on the stage. Anything of value will take hours and hours of grinding out the mistakes and polishing the final product.

Now, if you're thinking that you don't have time to practice, let me remind you of something. We all have the same 24 hours, the same 1,440 minutes, the same 86,400 seconds of the day. How do you use yours? Start a journal documenting your time each week. Find the leaks of time—the time you wasted doing what was not necessary for you to grow. This doesn't mean you can't still be a great parent or friend or partner. It will simply take the sacrifice of some of your "personal time."

Step Four: Perform

"To win any battle, you must fight as if you are already dead."
—Miyamoto Musashi

Performing is, simply put, the culmination of all of your preparation and practice. If you have done the required work as thoroughly as you can, then all you will need to go out and do is be you. When you allow your preparation and practice to come forth, you'll see results. This can go for a presentation, an interview, a client call, or simply going in and successfully completing a day's work.

I always slept soundly before games because I knew that I had done everything possible to ensure victory, and I trusted our coaching staff to have done the same. Because we had worked so hard during the week, our players were free to play to the best of their abilities.

I see too many people doubting themselves after they've put in the work. This is the worst thing you can do! If you don't believe in yourself, then how will anyone else? Often, someone who is nervous or scared hasn't put in the necessary work; they didn't grind those big problems down to the small pieces that allow them to have the foundation to be great.

When your time to show comes, you will find what was "nervousness" will be replaced by confidence. This positive energy will feel similar to the "butterflies" in your stomach, but when the game or show or presentation begins, you will find a peace that comes with great preparation. When you know your material and have taken every opportunity to make sure the stage is set, the performance is the fun part!

Step Five: Perseverance

"Step by step, walk the thousand-mile road."
—Miyamoto Musashi

What happens when you lose the game? When you don't get the job? When you don't get the client to come to your company? How do you respond?

I certainly haven't won every game I've played or coached. Michael Jordan didn't make every shot, Mike Trout doesn't hit a home run with every swing, and Tom Hanks doesn't get an Academy Award for every movie he does. Shit happens. What really matters is how you respond to the losses.

Do you persevere and continue the grind with the same positive attitude, or do you question your path and quit? I had this moment when I was the Associate Head Strength Coach at the University of Tennessee. I was up for the head strength coaching job at another college. I was told that I was the top guy on their list, and they would make it formal as soon as UT's season was over. In November of 2000, I was diagnosed with Hodgkin's disease. When this other university found out, I never heard from them again. In a matter of days, I found out I had a 40% chance to beat the cancer *and* I had lost out on a major college strength job.

But I didn't quit. I continued working through the chemo treatments, and in January, I received a call to be the head strength coach at the University of Southern California. The one question Pete Carroll asked me was, "Is the cancer going to make you a different coach?"

I'll bet you can guess my answer. But in case you can't, it was a resounding "NO!"

"Can you be here on Monday?" he replied.

I never missed a single day of work, and after 12 months, I was in remission. After five years, they said I was cancer-free.

Alexander Graham Bell once said, "As one door closes, another opens." And I am a living example. It wasn't about luck; it was about perseverance. Continuing to push forward until your opportunity comes. We really never know what's going to happen or what's on the other side; all we can do is control what we can and let go of the rest.

I fought through two seasons where I didn't win a single game as a coach. That didn't make me stop coaching. I just forced myself to be better. There have since been three seasons where we won every game.

Pursuing the Horizon

I recently found a poem that sums up this whole concept of perseverance. It was written by Stephen Crane, the author of the book *The Red Badge of Courage*. It's the only poem I have ever memorized. For one thing, it's short, and the title is the first line of the poem. But the most important reason is that it spoke to me. It goes like this:

I saw a man pursuing the horizon;
Round and round they sped.
I was disturbed by this;
I accosted the man.
"It is futile" I said
"You can never ---"
"YOU LIE" he cried,
and ran on.

I have found that fighting through all of the negativity is the answer to holding on and continuing to grind on your way to significance. In college, I was told by a person whom I saw as a "close friend" that I would never be successful in the coaching world. In some ways, he might have been right. As a head football coach, I was terrible! I own this fact. However, he was wrong. I have proven that I am very good at what I am very good at. And that is motivating people to do what they often never thought they could do. And if they thought they could be the best, I helped them to achieve their dreams.

I did it as a coach.

There is always someone who will tell you that whatever you are thinking about doing is futile, that you can't actually attain your dreams. Crane's protagonist simply told that person, "You lie!" and then ran on. I've spent my whole life chasing the dreams people constantly told me were futile. However, any good story has an antagonist. Without him, what would fuel the fire in the protagonist?

From a kid born with a physical handicap that led a doctor to tell my mom I would never run like the other boys, to the speech therapist who told my parents I would never be a public speaker, to the cancer that tried to derail my forward progress, to the daunting task of moving up the ladder in an attempt to be successful at the highest levels… I've had plenty of antagonists. And you know what?

I've proven every single one of them wrong along the way—the naysayers, the lazy, the jealous, the conniving backstabbers who wanted to see nothing more than for me to fail. They didn't (and still don't) know who I truly am. They didn't know I had this poem to cling to, giving me the drive to be the best at whatever I did.

My competitive edge does not burn like a bonfire, but like a furnace deep inside a steel factory. It is *constantly* burning hotter than a bonfire that can burn itself out—one that only burns when people are watching. That isn't me. I live on my own ambition. It was put there from the time I was first conceived. While some stoke it from time to time with their doubt in my ability to persevere, it is forever burning red-hot.

I constantly ask myself these questions:

How much can I do with the time that is at hand?

How relevant can I be?

How do I continue to make a difference in the lives of other people?

Who is going to be the next one to tell me what I can't do, so I can prove them wrong?

And I encourage *you* to do the same.

Don't Quit

There are examples in history, both bygone and present, of people who had every reason to get stuck in what they were doing and ultimately stagnate and cease maximizing their lives. One of the greatest men ever to live only became who he was supposed to be because he didn't quit. If Abraham Lincoln had given up after losing one of the eight elections that he lost before becoming president, where would this country be right now? His drive and energy would have been lost to this country in its darkest period. The way he pulled the country together after it had split was a super-human effort. If you look at pictures of Lincoln both before the election of 1860 and right before he was assassinated, you will see two very different people. He gave every fiber of himself to this country.

What if baseball player Ted Williams sat on the bench on the last day of the season instead of playing? His .3996 batting average would have been rounded up to a .400 batting average, but he would have always had that asterisk in that back of his head. Instead, he said he was playing that final day and ended the season with a .406 batting average. Would he have been seen as the greatest pure hitter in the history of baseball if he had sat on the bench? Would his .406 be held in the esteem that it is, being the last time a major league hitter ended the season batting .400 or more? This man could have taken the easy way out, but he chose to persevere and play on the final day of the season. This tells a lot about his competitive nature, knowing who he was, and trusting in his ability to get the job done.

Vera Wang worked for *Vogue* magazine. After 15 years as a senior fashion editor, she was passed over for the editor-in-chief position. She left the magazine industry and started her own clothing line, allowing her creativity to help carry her to where she was destined to be. She could have gotten down about the rejection, but instead, she did something about it. She maximized her potential and persevered after being told she wasn't good enough. She trusted her ability to put out high-quality clothing and didn't let the naysayers dissuade her from reaching her dreams.

There are stories all around us where people did not allow life to get them down and convince them to quit. These people found strength enough to push on and endeavor to be the best they can be. And they are no better or no worse than any of us!

The only difference is that they didn't *allow* themselves to quit on their dreams. Kris Richard once told me, "The amount of pain you can endure will be equal to the success you can expect to enjoy." If we keep these words in mind, we will overcome all the negativity that tries to hold us back.

The amount of pain you can endure will be equal to the success you can expect to enjoy.

Now, Get to Work!

Utilizing the Five Ps isn't rocket science. In fact, you only need to have your mind made up that the level of your success will be equal to the amount of time, effort, and sacrifice you are willing to make.

The first stage is the toughest. In order to have a positive attitude, you will need to have **passion** for whatever you do. It can't last a day or two, or even a month or so; it's got to be something that propels you forward your entire life. Your passion will make every day exciting. When the grind becomes long, you will need to be able to look ahead and remind yourself of the reasons it isn't an option for you to quit.

The next two stages (**prepare** and **practice**) are tough because no one is watching the hours you spend preparing, and very few people are watching you go through the practice. You must be internally motivated to work these stages at the highest level. Jimmy Johnson once said, "The difference between ordinary and extraordinary is that little extra." It sounds simple, but it is the wall that prevents most people from achieving their goals on the way to accomplishing their dreams.

Once you have committed yourself to excellence, the **performance** part of the equation is easy. It flows from you like water from a fire hose. Because you trusted the process of preparation and practice, you will have nothing to worry about because you will have already taken care of any issue that might attempt to trip you up!

Because we can't put an exact time on our lives, we will need to be vested in the grind. We will need to **persevere** through setbacks, losses, and even grind through success. Nothing will slow you down more than being successful early on, as it would be easy to become complacent. Accept you are on the right path and continue to grind.

Take the Risk

Mediocrity is self-inflicted. Greatness is self-bestowed.
—Walter Russell

"You need to go after that opportunity—hard!"

It was my immediate response when my good friend, Paul, called me about an opportunity that had just opened up. I knew a little bit about the organization, and I knew it was an opportunity he shouldn't pass up.

This kind of professional opportunity didn't open up very often, and it was perfect for him. I pushed and prodded and gave him positives for every negative that he gave me. I was glad that I was one of his four quarters. I totally believed in this guy. I knew his background and his abilities, and I knew it was the logical next step for him.

However, he thought it was a risky proposition. You see, he would have to risk the relative security that he had at present. But at that time, he was working in a position that didn't utilize his talents to their fullest. As our conversation was coming to a close, I could tell that I had not convinced him. The next day we talked again, and he admitted he had decided not to pursue the opportunity. I told him he did what was in his heart, so he couldn't be wrong.

A week later, he called because he was mad about the guy they had hired. And for good reason! The new hire was nowhere as qualified as my friend. He didn't have half the time in the profession and had very little prior success. Of course, Paul was now second-guessing his decision. I told him to simply pack those feelings up and use them to help him decide when the next opportunity came around.

Do you know what the biggest problem was in this situation? **He was afraid to risk what he had for what he might become.**

Another one of my friends, we'll call him Adam, was one of the brightest, sharpest minds in football. When I first met him, he had just left a graduate assistant's position at an SEC (Southeastern Conference) school. He was really good. Too qualified to be at the high school we were working at, in my opinion. Maybe you're wondering why it was OK for me to be coaching at the high school level and not him. The truth is I was fine—I was exactly where I "needed" to be at this time in my career. I was just trying to become as good as Adam was. Eventually, my guy would become the head coach at this high school. He was too good for that job, too. But while I moved on, he stayed.

Eventually, I had the opportunity to help Adam get into the college ranks again. I moved from Trinity Valley Community College to the University of Tennessee, which was a no-brainer move for me. I spoke to the head coach at TVCC, Scotty Conley, and he agreed that Adam would be a great replacement. In fact, I think he used the term "upgrade." Adam and Scotty talked a bit, and all was set for the position to be passed on to him. All Adam had to do was accept the opportunity. But he turned it down. He thought that maybe it was going to be the big year at the high school… the same one he had been at since we met.

As you might have guessed, it wasn't the big year. Nor the next, or the next. Eventually, the school wanted to move in a different direction, and Adam had to move on. He ended up leaving coaching altogether and got into the administrative side. I have no doubt that he is the best administrator there is because he's just that kind of guy.

But this is the classic "stuck, stagnate, die" scenario. He got stuck in a job that he was only going to be at until the next hiring cycle came around. Because of his competitiveness, Adam took the head coaching position. Though he had some good seasons, he kept looking down the road to the next season (and then the next season) to validate his sacrifice to stay. He eventually died professionally when he never got that "special season" where all his effort and commitment finally paid off on the scoreboard. Even when he was thrown one last lifeline, he turned it down.

He was afraid to risk what he had for what he might become.

Hear me out here: I'm not saying he wasn't successful because he never won the big game. But, in my estimation, he did not allow himself to climb the ladder in the profession that he was made for. I'm not advocating that you hop from job to job, either. But when one of your closest friends knows the ramifications of the move and the opportunities that will come from making said move, and you don't take it, then you are keeping yourself stuck. Soon you will only be seen as "that person"—an employee who is satisfied with where they are and stops trying to keep moving forward. Which is fine, if you felt comfortable having reached this position. However, is that *really* what you dreamt of as a 10-year-old? Did you wish to become average? Did you always want your hard work to be used to promote the people you worked for? Did you always want to see less qualified people move ahead of you?

The Good, the Bad and the Ugly

Over my career, I've had eight different coaching opportunities. I don't call them "jobs" because coaching and helping people along their path is more than just a job for me. It's a passion and an opportunity to help.

I came to understand my weaknesses, and instead of hiding them, I educated myself so I could be a better teacher to the young people I had the great opportunity to work with. I took risks—both financially and professionally—to climb the ladder to what I thought was the "end of my rainbow." The NFL. However, during the journey, my true "why" was revealed to me. It wasn't the winning of championships; it was helping people maximize their God-given potential.

As I moved along my own path to significance, I was confronted with choices about where I should take my next step. If I were to take a step that required a lot of risk, and it wasn't the right move, I may not be able to get back on my path for quite a while. In the beginning, I had fewer things to take into consideration. But as time went on, I needed to make sure I was taking *calculated* risks. To help with my decision-making process, I developed a risk assessment system that helped me take educated steps to get to where I wanted to be.

The risk assessment system has five steps:

1) Why did the opportunity open?

2) Whom will I be working with?

3) What is the good, the bad, and the ugly?

4) Can I make a difference?

5) How will this affect my family?

What follows is my resume of opportunities that took me from a Class C-2 high school in Nebraska to an NFL team in the Pacific Northwest. As I go through each opportunity, I want to highlight the parts of the risk assessment system I used throughout my career. Each step had both easy choices and some unexpected twists.

Opportunity #1: Dodge High School – Dodge, Neb. – Head Football Coach / Strength Coach:

My arrogance, ignorance, and inflexibility were strong at Dodge. The coach I replaced had been hired at a larger high school. I would be working with two veteran teachers/coaches named Ken Ippenson and Gordy Pilmore. Both knew more about EVERYTHING than I did. I was *arrogant* in thinking that I was ready to be a head coach,

I was *ignorant* in not asking for help from Ken and Gordy, and I was *inflexible* because I didn't think I was the problem. This opportunity was my first one right out of college, and I would have taken any head coaching job that would give me a chance. I thought I could make a difference because I thought I knew everything. The truth was that I didn't know what I didn't know, and I wasn't even trying to learn.

Opportunity #2: Blytheville High School – Blytheville, Ark. – Assistant Football / Track / Strength Coach:

The opportunity at Blytheville opened because the former assistant had moved on to a larger school. The staff was made up of several men I had been coached by in college, so I knew who they were going into this opening. The opportunity filled a professional demand, as I desperately needed to learn about coaching after discovering I didn't know a thing about it in my first professional outing. This staff had several members who had been in the coaching profession for 15 or more years, so I knew they would help me farther down the professional path. And I thought *I* could help the team because I was a hard worker. Since the school was in the South, it was culturally different than what I had grown up with in the Midwest, which was a great learning experience for me. I was single, so the move was straightforward. Everything I owned fit into my Mercury Lynx two-door with a broken driver's seat.

Opportunity #3: University of Arkansas – Fayetteville, Ark. – Graduate Assistant Strength & Conditioning Coach:

The previous GA I replaced had gone on to get a head coaching position in a college in Utah. I again knew some of the staff, which included two coaches by the names of John Stucky and Tim Weiss. These men were already established in the coaching profession, and I was ready to move from being a high school coach to a college opportunity. I felt the learning experience was a necessary step to continue to move up the coaching ladder. I also had the chance to earn my master's degree, which would benefit me if I continued to move on to college /

professional-level coaching (or if I went back to the high school level). I thought I knew everything about lifting weights since I had done it for several years, but once again, I was wrong. I did bring my loyalty and work ethic, however, which made up for my lack of knowledge. I was married, but we had no children, so we could make ends meet. I was making $400 a month for 10 months of the year, and rent was $450 a month for 12 months of the year. We went from putting money in the bank and living rent free to not making enough to pay rent. It was the last financial decision I made for my family, ever!

Opportunity #4: Subiaco Academy – Subiaco, Ark. – Head Football Coach / Strength & Conditioning Coach:

The previous coach at Subiaco had recently retired, and I was recommended for this opportunity by Joe Spivey, who was at the U of Arkansas in the sports academic area. The position was my last hurrah to see if I really could be a successful football coach. They had great facilities and a group of students who were incredibly hardworking. Being a boarding school, they were hungry for something to do with their time. The students who were locals came from great farm families; they knew how to *work*. So, with great facilities and hardworking kids—what more can you ask for? Well, maybe a few kids who could "get to the edge," but no opportunity is perfect. I felt the experience I had gained in my eight years of coaching could help build a successful program. My wife was glad I finally was getting paid, so it was an easy move.

Opportunity #5: Trinity Valley Community College – Athens, Texas – Offensive Line Coach / Strength & Conditioning Coach:

The previous coach at TVCC had moved up to a four-year college position, and I knew the head coach, Scotty Conley, from my time at the University of Arkansas. He was one of the smartest, most prepared, and organized coaches that I had ever met. He was always ready. I knew I would learn a ton from him. At Subiaco, I had learned what I wasn't: a head football coach. But I had also developed my training philosophy over my four years there. TVCC would turn out to be a great proving ground. I would be able to combine my two greatest passions: coaching the offensive line and strength. I knew my strength and conditioning background would be a huge benefit for this junior college team. Even though my weight room was a converted racquet-ball court, I knew I could make a difference. Scotty was such a great teacher on the field that he brought my coaching skills up to speed very quickly. This was another good move for my family. We still had no children, and TVCC paid better.

Opportunity #6: University of Tennessee – Knoxville, Tenn. – Associate Head Strength & Conditioning Coach:

The coach I replaced at UT had moved on to a head strength coach position. I was reunited with my mentor in the strength and con-ditioning profession, John Stucky. I knew I was not going to climb the ladder being a football coach. Though we had won the JUCO National Championship in the one season I was at TVCC, I still felt my calling was going to be in the weight room and the preparation of the athletes. I knew I could help John continue to develop players that would give the football coaches the tools they would need to be successful. The step up from a junior college to a Division I SEC school was a no-brainer. On the home front, we lost our shirt in the sale of the house. We bought and refurbished a house in June and sold it in December. Real estate lesson: it's hard to make a profit in six months, but it was the right move to make to get to where we wanted to be.

Opportunity #7: University of Southern California – Los Angeles, Calif. – Head Strength & Conditioning Coach:

The coach I replaced at USC was only removed because the head football coach wanted to bring "his own guy" in to run the strength & conditioning area. Coach Stucky was very familiar with the head football coach, Pete Carroll, having worked with him in the past, and knew it was an opportunity that I could make better. USC was a head strength coaching opportunity, it was in a major college, and it had been down on its luck for a while, which made it a prime candidate for me to help rejuvenate with a new training philosophy. I had been diagnosed with cancer in November, and the job offer came in January. I was sure that I could muster the energy to do the work I knew would have to be done. I made sure that no one other than the head football coach knew of my health situation so that I wouldn't be coddled. I knew with my 16 years of experience that I had answers to some of the questions I would face. My training philosophy—the one that I had developed at Subiaco and refined at TVCC and UT—would help to develop the athletes this team would need to be successful. The weight room space was the worst in the conference… and maybe the country! I had no illusions that it would change soon, so I wasn't tricked by the "opulence of the palace." My wife and I had a son, Alex, who was a year and a half when I took the job. He didn't even know we moved.

Opportunity #8: Seattle Seahawks – Seattle, Wash. – Head Strength & Conditioning Coach:

Much like USC, I replaced the former head strength coach in Seattle because Pete Carroll felt more comfortable with me running his preparation program. Coming into an NFL opportunity, he knew he had other fires to tend to, so with the weight room being under the control of a guy he trusted, there was at least one area he wouldn't have to change. The job was at the top of my list; it seemed like my "end of the rainbow" job. The one I had always dreamt of. I knew I would succeed. I trusted myself and my assistants, Mondray Gee and Jamie Yanchar, to put together a program that would keep us at the top of our game. This move was the hardest on my family. After nine years in SoCal, my wife had made great friends, and my son was leaving the only friends he had grown up with. We now have Riley, our dog, which was a bribe I made to my son to sweeten the move. You promise what you need to sometimes!

Risk Assessment System: Going Through My Choices

I now want to walk you through the system I created that allowed me to walk through each of those moves gracefully and successfully, which I hope you'll take and make your own as you move along your path to significance.

1.   Why did the opportunity open?

Each job had a logical reason for the opportunity to come open. The previous coach had moved up in the profession, retired, or had been a casualty of the coaching profession.

2.   Whom will I be working with?

I had a good idea of whom I would be working with in each program. Several times, I found mentors through these positions. John Stucky, Scotty Conley, Father William Wewer, Tim Weiss, and Father Jerome Kodell all helped me get better in coaching and be a better person. Each progression had its positives and negatives, but the positives far outweighed the latter. In every opportunity, people come and people go, and you can learn from them all. The one thing you can't have is to enter into a hostile work environment where you are the "bad guy" as soon as you walk in the door, which is why you must do your homework.

3.   The Good, the Bad, and the Ugly

The Good: What benefit is there in going to the new job? I needed to know that this opportunity was going to move me farther along my professional and personal path. Even though some of the moves look like they were a step backward, especially from the head coach at Dodge to an assistant's position at Blytheville, they were actually strategic moves necessary to prepare me to continue making positive moves.

The Bad: Why are you leaving your current situation? Can it be fixed? Too many people move just for the sake of moving. However, the job they are going to won't advance them to where they want to be. Once they make these moves and their coaching resume gets tarnished because they were just bad opportunities, they need to get back to where they once were. There was never a move on my resume that was made on a whim. Each opportunity was a step in a positive direction. There were many opportunities that I passed on because they didn't put me in a better position.

The Ugly: Are you being enticed to look at the new job by surface optics? When I'm talking about "surface optics," I am referring to the first look you get. If an opening looks too good to be true, it probably is. If the person who held the job before you took a lateral move to leave the job opening, then it probably isn't the best place to move. Make sure you look behind the "curtain" when you are shown the shiny part of an opportunity. When I was coaching in college, our facilities had terrible leaks from the patio above the weight room and the meeting rooms. The water would pour into buckets, and the wallpaper in the meeting room areas would peel off the wall. When recruits would come in, we would have the landscaper not water the plant boxes and hang tarps blocking the hallways to cover up the water damage. It was all about the optics. Don't fall into this issue, my friend. Go in with full knowledge of what you're going to be dealing with. In my case, the jobs that had bad weight rooms weren't a big deal to me. I didn't need all the bells and whistles to develop athletes. I just needed willing subjects and space.

4. Can I make a difference?

I would hate to go into an opportunity following a "legend." That's a tough situation. If a program was really successful and the head coach moves on or retires, you will only be continuing what was done before you. People will often look at your accomplishments and say, "You just didn't screw up a good thing." I want to be the one who breaks up the sod and gets the farm back on its feet. I took this idea from my father. He climbed from a rail-pounding crew when he began working with the railroad to the position of Assistant Vice President of the entire railroad before he retired. He climbed the ladder by taking all of the "bad jobs" and turning them into great opportunities. He didn't want it easy; in fact, the harder, the better. That is how he left his mark. He made a difference because he trusted himself, and his company benefitted from his hard work.

5. How will this affect my family?

Though this is the last one on the list, it became my first concern when I got married and started a family. When you decide you need to make a move, you need to consult with your "home team"—your family. My wife, Louon, is the quintessential coach's wife. She is smart, independent, and driven. She understands the profession, the time alone because of the brutal hours, and the emotional swings that occur during the season. Even though moves like the one to the University of Arkansas were economically stressful, we knew it was a short-term move with long-lasting, positive repercussions. When your "team" is on board, you can handle anything.

I developed this risk assessment system several years down my career path. There is no way I would have been able to see a pattern had I not gone through it myself. After the first few moves, I started to see the same things, and I asked myself the same questions each time. Eventually, I was able to formulate a bank of questions that amounted to hurdles an opportunity would have to clear for it to be a viable consideration. Soon, it became a "system" that I would lean on when I was trying to make decisions to take an opportunity or to let the opportunity pass by. It worked well enough that I can't say that I made a professional mistake in any opportunity that I took because I took the biggest risks out of the equation.

Perspective is Everything

With age, we get perspective. We are able to look back over the life we've lived and start to connect the dots—the things we did right, and the things we could have done without. Don't try to polish the truth. Look back at your work history. When you moved from a bad situation to a better one, give yourself credit. But when you made a bad professional move, own it and learn from it. By analyzing our past, we can start to understand patterns. We can see when we are successful or where we have slowed our progress. When we understand the reason we are where we are right now, we can move forward. If we don't own our strengths and weaknesses, we will continue to make the same mistakes. However, when we apply the truth of who we are to a proven system, we can start to reduce the professional risks we have to take in order to get to where we dream to be.

I wish every step I took in my professional career was the right decision, but like the majority of people, there are several things I wish I could change as I look back. Since this is the real world, and I can't go back and start over, all I can do is apologize for those I have hurt and make sure that I respond differently in the future. I make sure that in every situation where I made a less-than-perfect decision, I choose to turn it into a learning experience.

One of the first risks I took was when I was still in college. At the end of my senior football season in high school, I was offered a college scholarship to play football at a junior college, North Iowa Area Community College (NIACC). I was looked at by other larger schools, but everyone agreed that I would need to put on size, as I was a 6'1" lineman who weighed 185 pounds. The large schools felt I had potential but needed time to grow. So, the junior college scholarship route was the best way to go. I could have risked walking onto a larger school, but I loved actually playing the game—not just practicing all week with no opportunity to play for two or three years, if ever.

After one season at NIACC, I received a scholarship offer to a Division II school, Chadron State College (CSC). I had a choice: I could turn down the offer and risk staying one more season at NIACC in hopes that I would continue to grow and possibly earn a scholarship to a larger school, or I could take the new opportunity. The thing that ultimately tipped my decision was that CSC was a "teachers' school." Though they have several areas of learning, CSC is widely known for the quality of the teachers they turn out. At the time, my career plan was to play college football and become a teacher and a coach. This is where the adage "One in the hand is worth two in the bush" came into play in real life.

I knew who I was as a football player. I was good, but I wasn't great. So, I jumped at the opportunity to go to a level where I could compete *and* earn a teaching degree. With the risk minimized and the opportunities maximized, I packed up the red Chevy Chevette and headed west to Chadron, Nebraska. Because of that choice, I was put into a position to be hired at my first job, Dodge High School. I was hired partly because of the reputation that Chadron had of turning out well-prepared teachers.

From these humble beginnings, other opportunities started to line up, and my risk assessment system began to develop. You see, much of life comes together without us knowing about it while it's happening. But when we take time to look back at our path, we will start to see how things came together. Many times, we'll find that what we were doing was just a vehicle to get us where we were supposed to end up.

Many times, we'll find that what we were doing was just a vehicle to get us where we were supposed to end up.

Is This Really It?

I worked in the coaching profession for 35 years, chasing what I *thought* was my passion: winning championships. Somewhere towards the end of my run—well, actually, I can pinpoint the day, February 3, 2014—I was sitting on the tarmac on the team plane after winning Super Bowl XLVIII the previous evening. The team was in the back of the plane recovering from the post-game celebration, and I was in my seat poring over the off-season program I had started to draw up during the previous six months. The program I was working on wasn't going to be used until mid-April. I celebrated the win for a total of 12 hours, then I was back doing what I did best: preparing athletes to maximize their potential.

Our takeoff was delayed for several hours because of a blizzard, so I had a lot of time to finish my work. When I had dotted the final "i" and crossed the final "t," I sat back and let out my breath. As I leaned back in my seat, I started to worry about the next season. I looked around to see some of the coaches laughing and talking while others slept off the overindulging from the night before. I felt disconnected. I'm wondering if Sir Edmund Hillary had the same feeling after climbing Mount Everest with Tenzing Norgay.

"Is that really it?"

I had dreamt of winning championships my whole life. I had succeeded in winning a championship at every level of organized football, and my hunger still wasn't satiated.

I would wrestle with this for the rest of the off-season and the next. The 2014 season cemented my feelings. We went to the Super Bowl again, and though we lost, I still sat on the tarmac in Phoenix, finishing the off-season program. A year earlier, I could move past winning quickly, but this loss—well, actually, any loss—was a different story. The Super Bowl loss hung on me like the loss to the University of Texas for the collegiate national championship still does to this day. The previous victories in championship games rolled off in minutes but losing never leaves.

Somewhere in 2015, I finally came to understand who I was truly created to be. I wasn't in the game because of the wins. The wins were nice, don't get me wrong, but I wasn't in the game for those. I was in the game to help others achieve their dreams. It was the grandest epiphany ever to strike me.

The previous revelations of who I actually was had come like lightning bolts as well. On the school bus, driving home after a loss to Norfolk Catholic, I came to understand I didn't know shit about being a football coach. The second epiphany came when I finally understood that I didn't need to yell to teach others how to maximize their potential. The third was when I realized my calling to help others was as a *strength coach*, not a football coach.

Though I didn't realize it at the time, every one of those scenarios was teaching me the same thing: Coaching was simply a vehicle I was using to accomplish my greatest passion of helping people reach their true potential.

My Next Move

I was about to go through a professional transition at the ripe age of 55, but I was OK with it. I have always trusted my ability to do whatever it was I set my mind on. So, I simply followed my normal procedure when faced with a new opportunity: I went through my risk assessment.

The opportunity opened up because I finally realized that though I could help a hundred people during a football season, I could help thousands through public speaking and coaching. As I went through my questions, the first thing I realized was that I wasn't replacing anyone. I was finally working for myself. I only needed to impress one person, but that person knew me better than anyone and wouldn't let me slow down! Some would see this as a good thing, but you don't know me like I know me. I am relentless in the way I go about my professional endeavors. The person I was "working for" was going to be less forgiving than any other boss had ever been. But it was a risk I was willing to take.

Moving down the line with my risk assessment and charting out the good, the bad, and the ugly, I found that one of the benefits was that I would get to do something I had always loved to do. I had the privilege to work with those who had never been spoken to like I had spoken to athletes. I was coaching people who may have never been in the sports environment, instilling energy and belief in them that had never seen the light of day.

I wasn't so much leaving coaching; I just wasn't affiliated with a team anymore. I had no "borders" on whom I could speak to. No company rules on what I could or couldn't talk about. I could speak to men and women. I could speak to young people, successful people, and people searching for a helping hand. I began to speak to local civic groups and then groups of bankers and real estate professionals, and then on to large corporations, colleges, and commencement ceremonies. And I loved it.

The opportunity passed the next piece of the risk assessment with flying colors as well. My family was 100% behind me, and we decided it was time to leave Seattle. We sold our house and left town. After nine years in the Pacific Northwest, we had begun to grow webbing between our toes with all of the rainy days. All I needed was an airport and some sun, so we headed south, which also allowed me to help my brother Steve and his wife Tammy take care of our father.

My risk assessment boxes were all checked as I prepared for this new opportunity. Once we got settled, I joined a local Toastmasters group that helped me learn how to develop speeches and present a meaningful talk. I knew I would need help in getting started, so I reached out to my four quarters and friends I had made during my coaching career. These people then pushed me down the path of my transitional period, keeping me moving down the line.

One such connection I made was while I was coaching at USC. One spring, a skinny school newspaper reporter named Ben Malcolmson was doing a story on the USC football team. He had spoken with the head football coach, Pete Carroll, about doing the story from the inside. They agreed to have him go through the tryout phase prior to spring practice. Ben wrote stories about his experiences that then expanded to the summer preparation phase and into the season. Ben writes about this in his book *Walk On*.

He went on to become Pete's right-hand man in building connections outside of football and became an author; today, he is a great friend. Ben connected me with Bryan and DeeDee Heathman, who run the publishing company that helped me get connected to Katie Rios, my editor. This is how I got to where I am today—exactly where I am supposed to be.

Because I took a calculated risk that, in the short term, was a struggle, I trusted myself and played the long game. I was able to accomplish everything I had ever dreamt of. I didn't blindly jump from opportunity to opportunity. Each step was a step that I needed to take to develop my philosophy (and myself) for what was coming. Each move added more "arrows" to my quiver of knowledge. I was able to watch the best teachers teach and the greatest coaches coach. I also saw the worst part of the profession in many of the coaches I worked with. I think one of the most valuable things I learned was not only how to do things better, but more importantly, how NOT to do things.

As we attempt to minimize risks in our professional life, we must begin by trusting our strengths. From here, we can create our own roadmap of how we are going to get where we want to be. But the map doesn't necessarily have to be specific. I didn't know how taking the head coaching position at Subiaco would get me to the NFL, but I knew I needed the experience and the time to develop my system of training to get anywhere I wanted to be. The important thing is that I trusted I was on the right path to maximize my abilities.

Do you need to step out and take a calculated risk to get to where you want to be? Now's the time to assess the situation and make your move. What are you waiting for?

Chapter 7

The Road Less Traveled

> Two roads diverged in a wood, and I—I took the one less traveled by, And that had made all the difference.
> —Robert Frost

Too many people see creative thinkers as troublemakers. Risk takers. Rebels. Many people *talk* about doing it. Some even dip their toes in the ocean of questioning what has been done before, but they don't fully dive into a seemingly risky venture. They are happy with being stuck doing things like everyone else. Remember our first chapter? Often, these types of people don't have any idea how to make things better (ignorance), they think they are doing things better than they've ever been done before (arrogance), or they don't think that they need to change or they're too lazy to risk expanding the walls of the box they have been born into (inflexibility).

Or… it might be that they simply trust themselves enough to walk a different path. In Robert Frost's epic poem, "The Road Not Taken," the last three lines give us all the push that we need to keep moving down the line to significance.

"Two roads diverged in a wood, and I –
I took the one less traveled by,
And that has made all the difference."

"And that has made all the difference." Taking the other path presented risks, but the one more traveled presented its own risks—that of ending up in the same place as everyone else.

When I developed my training regimen with a central philosophy being "movement," I was taking a risk. Strength and conditioning at that time was just that—lifting weights and running. My decision to make lifting *one* of the five areas of training (speed, agility, power, endurance, and strength) rather than the most important was seen as near-heresy. Instead of spending 80% of my workout in the weight room, I was now spending 80% of my work time training the athletes to move more efficiently, more explosively, and faster. It helped propel the last five teams that I worked with to championships.

I wasn't the only one who took football down a less-traveled path. Over the last 10 to 15 years, the landscape of college football has changed dramatically. In 2007, Chip Kelly brought a wide-open, no-huddle offensive philosophy to the University of Oregon. This offensive concept has been copied and mutated several times by other coaches around college football. "Fast break" football is now leeching into the professional ranks, in contrast to the old pattern of trends starting in the NFL and disseminating to college.

There's an old saying attributed to Ralph Waldo Emerson: "If you build a better mousetrap, the world will beat a path to your door." Chip Kelly didn't necessarily invent the system, but he gave it national attention. He was thinking outside the box. He had run the system in a smaller setting, at the University of New Hampshire, where it had become roadworthy. And then he took it on the highway to the University of Oregon, and it worked just as well. I had gone through the same process with my program. I took it from Subiaco to TVCC to Tennessee. When I got to USC and Seattle, it was a finely oiled machine. Each step took a little of the risk out of the process.

As we stray away from "the box"—the way things have been done before—we need to continue to test our hypothesis throughout the developmental process. Most good ideas on paper don't always run as smoothly on the hard pavement. When I was at the University of Tennessee, we had a great group of graduate assistants (GAs), part-time paid coaches, and volunteer strength coaches. These were hardworking, young, intelligent coaches who were active in the weight room. If we had an idea that we might want to implement in our existing program, we would have the GAs add our changes to their workout regimen. If they began having negative responses to the new program, we could then make the appropriate changes. When we eventually got the kinks worked out of the program, we knew we could safely add it to our athletes' programs.

This is just one simple example of calculating risks in order to minimize the possible errors in planning that are introduced into the pipeline.

There are always limits to thinking outside the box. Just because something is different doesn't necessarily make it *better*. Every business has that sect of people who feel they aren't a big enough cog in their company's machine. To get the attention they hunger for, they will throw idea after idea up against the corporate wall, hoping something (anything) will stick. They will promise miraculous results in their attempt to be on the "cutting edge." Think about a venture capitalist who inherited millions of dollars from his family, or a marketing professor who has never ventured outside the confines of his classroom. Though what they have to say might sound good, their principles haven't been tested in the real world.

> **If you build a better mousetrap, the world will beat a path to your door.**
> **—Ralph Waldo Emerson**

As a "professional watcher," I have learned my most impactful lessons by watching people do one of two things: succeed or fail miserably. I have always made it a habit to record these events in my research and development notebooks. These books contain the evolution of my training program. The notes on training progressions, seasonal cycles and deviations within a training cycle have helped me to develop a program that has been very successful. I found that this process ensured my success along each step of my professional journey.

I call this process the Five R's. These steps aided in making sure the process of introducing ideas had been tested thoroughly by me and my staff before they were introduced in a team setting. Thinking outside the box is a great process when done under a controlled system of checks and balances.

Recognize: Understand There is a Problem

The first stage of thinking outside the box is to **recognize** that there is a problem at hand. Whether it is with a process, a management philosophy, or a training program, if you want to make things better, you will have to first find and recognize the problems.

The longer you work in a profession, the more you will find that there are accepted flaws in the system. "That's the way we have always done it" is the most common excuse you'll hear. However, sometimes a fresh set of eyes with a different perspective can see that there is a better way. As you see a need for change, educate yourself on what has been tried in the past. Nobody wants to be seen as one "reinventing the wheel."

Oftentimes, people become comfortable in the system that they are using. When I got into coaching, especially on the strength and conditioning side of the profession, I saw the job of a strength coach completely differently than how it was perceived at the time.

When I took a good hard look into the preparation of athletes, I wondered why so many programs spent so much time in the weight room doing movements that weren't specific to the improvement of their athletes' ability to move in space (athleticism). In these programs, the time spent in the weight room is 80% of the total training time and working on movement is only given 20% of the time allotted for the strength and conditioning program during a normal work week. Does a team need weightlifters, or does it need better athletes? Of course, the answer is simple: Every coach at any level of sport will always trade improved athleticism over maximal strength. To make the changes that I felt needed to be made, I began to ask myself one of the hardest questions: "Why?"

Why are athletes spending most of their time in the weight room?

Why are we not doing movement drills that mimic the sport that we are preparing to play?

Why are we so concerned with "how much" and less concerned with "how to" and "how fast"?

Once I had become immersed in the problem, I couldn't help myself—I desperately needed to find the answers.

Research: Find Answers to the Problems

To make the changes I felt were necessary, I would need to search out the answers to my "why" questions. So, I swallowed my pride and went on a quest to learn about every aspect of movement I possibly could. Which brings me to the second stage of thinking outside the box: **researching** to find the answers to the problems.

I spoke at length with the great sprint coaches, Vince Anderson and Loren Seagrave. I visited Olympic lifting guru Steve Javorek to understand why a football player needed to do Olympic lifting movements and which part of the movement was the most important to get the most value on the football field. I read everything that Jim Radcliffe wrote and went to every clinic he spoke at to learn about plyometrics (jumping and explosive movements). I met up with physical therapists to learn about balance and body awareness. I listened to everything about the core (abdominal and lower-back strength) from the top back surgeon in the world, Dr. Robert Watkins.

I also took myself out of the sports world and used my background in history to study the writing of all of the great movement warriors and soldiers in world history. Alexander the Great, Hannibal, William Wallace, Shaka Zulu (kaSenzangakhona), Crazy Horse, Heinz Guderian, and George Patton. While studying the lives of these brilliant men, I came to understand the idea of *creating* chaos by training my athletes to be faster so that they could live *within* the chaos come game time.

Now that I had answers to the questions, I needed somewhere to put all of the answers. So, I created a program that would allow my athletes to play at a higher level—simple as that.

Receptive: Find Fertile Ground

In order to continue the process of thinking outside the box, you will need to move through the third phase and find a place that is **receptive**. A receptive organization or company is open to new ideas, which I liken to fertile ground. Now, in this case, sometimes bigger is not always better. You see, if you make mistakes in a small setting, the negative impact is smaller. This is the "calculated" part of taking the risk to think outside the box.

In my case, my resume wasn't good enough to get me into a large university, or even a small university… or even into a large high school, for that matter! But I *was* given the opportunity in the best testing ground in the world: Subiaco Academy.

At Subiaco, I didn't have great athletes. But that was OK; I didn't need great athletes. The one commodity that I *did* have was a group of young people who weren't afraid of a little hard work. In fact, I had that in bushels!

For four years, I was able to put together training programs that increased the athletic ability of normal, run-of-the-mill high school kids. I had them running and jumping and changing directions and lifting for the right reasons. No bells and whistles, just hard work.

At the end of my four years at Subiaco, I knew I had something special, but I needed to see how it would work in a larger setting.

Reach: Grow the Seed

Once you have a viable idea that has had the opportunity to stand on its own and still thrive, you will need to find a place to continue to test your process. In the fourth stage of thinking outside the box, you'll need to **reach** for another opportunity to grow.

My opportunity came when Scotty Conley asked me to join him as the offensive line and strength coach at Trinity Valley Community College located in Athens, Texas.

I jumped at the chance to put my program to the test in a larger setting. And the results were impressive. The athletes responded incredibly well to the training program. Throughout the season, the young men worked hard and continued to give me more information about my program through both their successes and failures.

I would take this information and continue to work on making my program complete.

At the end of that season, I was asked to rejoin John Stucky at the University of Tennessee. This was a large step up from where I had begun, but I was ready—and so was my program. This was Coach Stucky's program, and I was his associate head coach. My job was to give him solid answers when he asked me. So, I slowly implemented parts and pieces of my program into the existing one.

Though I could not introduce my program in its entirety, I used my time at UT to learn more and more by asking smarter people questions.

At the end of three seasons, I felt it was time to take another step forward in my professional career.

React: The Evolution of New Ideas

Now that your idea has been road tested and proven, you will need to continue to move your ideas forward. You may want to expand into larger markets or other industries, which may bring you into new, unfamiliar frontiers. This is where you need to tread lightly and move into the fifth phase of thinking outside the box: **reacting** to change.

In January of 2001, I received an offer to become the head strength and conditioning coach at the University of Southern California.

The athletes did a great job of adapting to what I was asking for. As I had mentioned, in most programs, 80% of the time was spent in the weight room. With my program, however, only 20% was based on the traditional weightlifting movements of benching and squatting. The other 80% was based on developing and increasing the athletic ability of the young athletes I was blessed to work with.

We had a great nine-year run at USC. But by my second year at USC, I was a little too far out of the box in my thinking of how to develop athletes for most people. This happens sometimes. When you get ahead of the pertinent research and training ideas, you find yourself in risky territory. But if you've calculated the risk properly, it's one worth taking.

For example, I used aspects of static stretching in my warm-up routine. The naysayers threw rocks at my program because studies had shown that long periods of static stretching diminished power and speed output. But no one had done studies that followed my warm-up routine, which consisted of a mix of active stretch, static stretch, and dynamic movement, all in short periods of use (about 10-15 seconds). Those who tried to tear my program apart only looked at studies that used static stretching for 60-90 seconds of duration, rather than the combination of static and dynamic flexibility and mobility movements that made up my warm-up. They were throwing the baby out with the bathwater, trying to prove their point while downplaying the success that my program had seen for over 25 years with 5 different teams in 4 different levels of competition.

As I moved to the forefront of the profession, I began to focus more on weighing the risks and rewards of my ideas.

Out of this thinking came the concept of moving away from maximum lifting. How much players lifted did not make them more agile. Actually, the opposite is true. The heavier they lift, the more mass they develop, the more baggage they have to carry, and the more slowly they move. I stopped doing strength testing and adopted a thought process of "strong enough." Is the athlete strong enough to compete at the highest level? This meant that I needed to know exactly where each of my athletes was during his daily work. I was working harder and smarter. Too many people want to rely on computers to do their thinking. For me and my staff, we were the computers! We didn't have to analyze data at the end of the day; we analyzed the information as it was happening and made changes immediately.

In 2010, I was asked to be the head strength coach of the Seattle Seahawks in the NFL. Would my program be able to fit into the NFL? It was another risky proposition I had to weigh, as I was also asked to stay at USC. It would be safe to stay, and I knew my program worked. But I took the risk and went with the Seahawks… and it worked there, too.

The difference between other coaches and me is that I actually saw my program as a living entity. It was constantly evolving and adapting as new ideas and new experiences were plugged in. The program did its job in keeping the athletes prepared at the highest level so they could continue to accomplish their dreams, regardless of the arena.

> **The difference between other coaches and me is that I actually saw my program as a living entity.**

My Five Rs

When the decision was made for me to move away from being a professional coach, I was ready for it. I had come to understand my true passion: Helping others to live their optimal life. Football had been a tremendous vehicle for this for 35 years. But I was limited in the number of people I could affect in a calendar year. Becoming a motivational speaker seemed risky to some who knew me as only a coach and had never heard me speak. To me, however, this was a calculated risk worth taking. I love speaking to new groups and seeing the excitement in their eyes as I talk about accomplishing their dreams.

I have followed my five Rs through my transition from strength coach to motivational speaker at the ripe young age of 57 years old. First, I **recognized** that I had the ability to get people to do what they didn't think they could so they could become who they wanted to become—I had a solution for their problems.

I **researched** this profession by watching videos and reading books from all the great motivational speakers: Craig Valentine, Jeannie Robertson, Patricia Fripp, Les Brown, and Eric Thomas. I also joined my local Toastmasters group to continue working on being a better speaker.

I found **receptive** audiences as a coach when I was allowed to give motivational presentations in a team setting before we would travel. I also had the opportunity to speak at 25-30 coaching clinics, which helped me become comfortable speaking in front of larger groups. I then moved out of the coaching domain and began speaking to civic clubs and other local organizations. This helped me to form my own unique speaking rhythm and style. I'll never forget how it feels to see the looks on the faces of people who have never experienced being "coached up" to change their lives.

Then, I began to **reach** farther as a speaker, accepting invitations to speak to businesses, corporations, and at commencement events. I found that my stories were unique to these groups. Too many people had come into their companies telling the same stories to make their points. My stories were unique in that they were MY stories, mostly about the way I had failed and then how I went about changing myself so I would be able to rise to the next challenge.

And now, I am in the **react** stage. I found that after I spoke, I would constantly be asked if I had a book out so that they could learn more. Sadly, I didn't. I was a one-off speaker: Hit 'em hard and move on to my next talk. However, when COVID started to eliminate my opportunities to help others, I knew it was time to write a book.

Now, I'm not the only one to go through these phases. People think outside the box and take calculated risks all the time! Here are a few examples of those who changed our lives by their risk-taking and new ways of thinking.

Taking Flight

I came across a couple of risk-takers after venturing into the Wright Brothers exhibit at the Smithsonian Institution's National Air and Space Museum in Washington, D.C. There in front of me was the Wright Flyer (also known as the Kitty Hawk Flyer), the air machine that the Wright brothers had flown over the dunes at Kitty Hawk, North Carolina. Since I love history, I was in heaven surrounded by facts and stories shown in cases and exhibits that circled the motorized glider made of canvas and wood.

Now, you should know that I am *always* searching for an unusual fact. And, of course, I found it there. In one of the small exhibits, there was a picture of John Smeaton. John Smeaton was a jack of all trades in the middle and late 18th century in England. He was a mechanical engineer, a physicist, and, most notably, he was called the "father of civil engineering." A really smart guy. In 1759, he published a paper entitled "An Experimental Enquiry Concerning the Natural Powers of Water and Wind to Turn Mills and Other Machines Depending on Circular Motion." I haven't read it… yet.

OK, I probably won't get around to it, but trust me when I say that out of this paper came the Smeaton coefficient. A coefficient is a "constant factor of a term as distinguished from a variable" (Merriam-Webster). The Smeaton coefficient was used in early flight mathematics to determine the effect that airflow had on the lift and drag upon a plane's wing.

Quickly: Can you tell me how many successful flights occurred from 1760 to 1903? If your answer is more than zero, you are incorrect. Early flight engineers used the Smeaton coefficient of 0.005, but it was wrong. The data that had been accepted for nearly 150 years was incorrect! It was garbage in, garbage out in *real life*. Now, I am not saying the Smeaton coefficient is garbage altogether. I'm sure it has value, but not in flight. Using a wind tunnel, the Wright brothers found the true coefficient to be 0.0033.

The Wright brothers thought outside the box. They looked at the problem and decided they would question every step of the mathematics of flight and test them all. And they were right. Going away from the accepted Smeaton coefficient was risky, but they trusted their research and their calculations. They were betting their lives on this, so imagine how much they believed in going out on their own in this area!

Because they risked everything, they are responsible for resetting the mathematics for flight—something we take for granted every time we step onto a plane to travel from one place to another. Moving away from a safe harbor is hard to do, but if you continue on the same path as everyone else, you may never live up to your potential. It kind of puts in perspective how thinking outside the box can be beneficial not only for you in your present situation but also for the rest of the industry. It isn't a risk if you know all of the variables; it's only a risk if you didn't do your research and testing!

Outside the Music Box

You want another one? Alright. Remember Eddie Van Halen? What about Eddie, other than his passing, had a profound effect on many of our lives? What about his style of playing the guitar?

Eddie had grown up around music. His brother was also a talented musician, most known for his time as a drummer in the brothers' band Van Halen. If you haven't introduced yourself to Van Halen, you need to stop reading right now and download some of their music.

I'll wait.

Eddie never learned to write or read sheet music—you know, the stuff with bars and dots and squiggly lines that describe and represent what the musician is doing. But that's not even the best part. The real "thinking outside the box" moment came when Eddie started tapping on the strings, adding a new dimension to the music world. It may be argued that others had tapped on a guitar before Eddie, but not to the extent that he did. It became so popular that the people who compose sheet music had to develop a brand-new written form to describe what Eddie did so effortlessly!

It was a huge risk to change the way he played the guitar. It could have ended the musical career (and subsequently, the dreams) of the Van Halen brothers. But they were so obsessed with the sound that they pushed it forward. Eddie Van Halen could have stayed with the mainstream picking and strumming the guitar, but he decided to walk with Robert Frost on that other path, which made all the difference.

Trendsetters

Thinking outside the box doesn't just happen in business and music. This phenomenon is happening all around us. Take Jason Belmonte, for example. By 2019, Belmonte had 11 major championships to his name and 22 Professional Bowlers Association (PBA) titles. He has bowled 23 perfect games and has been selected as Player of the Year five times in his career.

I know, I know. You're probably wondering what made this guy a "think outside the box" kind of guy.

I'm sure you have seen someone bowl before. They place three fingers of one hand in the ball, take a few steps, and then roll the ball down the alley, trying to knock as many pins down as possible. Jason found that he was a good bowler using this technique. The same technique used by all of the other professional bowlers. But Jason didn't want to be just good; he wanted to be the *best*.

Belmonte broke down his game and found that when he used just one arm, there were too many variants in the swing. Jason reverted back to a style he used when he was younger. He couldn't hold the ball with just one hand, so he added his other hand to the ball. This technique was the tipping point of his career. Once he perfected the two-handed release, he rid himself of the multiple variants and could control the ball's path better.

Sure, he risked looking different. Weird, even. But he looked at his strength and decided that if looking different allowed him to achieve his dreams, he was glad to do it.

Isn't it comical that one day you can look weird, and then the next you are a trendsetter?

Doing Things Better

Notice that Frost didn't say, "Follow the same old beaten-down path, and that will make the difference." Emerson didn't say, "If you build the same mousetrap as everyone else." He said, "If you build a *better*…"

If you want to do something better, the only way to do so is to take the risk.

Every aspect of our lives will present a risk at some point or another. When going through a transition as you move towards your optimal end—the achievement of your dreams and a life of significance—it is important to assess the risk you need to take. Nothing is worse than looking back to see that you veered off your path because you reacted too quickly.

Too many times, we don't fully trust ourselves or our strengths as we assess or take risks. If we have worked hard to understand who we are, we will have minimized some of them already. When we add to that the utilization of our unique strengths, the scale begins to sway in our direction as our talents begin to outweigh risks that make us question our decisions to make a change.

And, of course, we can reduce risk by going through the Five Rs we just learned. When I went against the system at hand and changed the preparation for athletes, I used these five steps. However, I only understood these steps after I had spent some time gaining perspective. Because I had the experience of developing a championship program, utilizing the Five Rs in building my motivational career came a lot easier. That's the great thing about perspective. It gives us a roadmap to who we are now.

Thinking outside the box should be at the forefront of everything we do. When you want to change the world, when you want to be the best at whatever you want to be, you can't do it by doing what everyone before you has done.

In the end, the risk may not be as big as you thought it was going to be—and the reward is going to be more than worth it.

Chapter 8

Leave Your Mark

Be so good that they can't ignore you.
—Steve Martin

In 1922, three teenagers named Marthe David, Andre David, and Henri Dutetre were exploring a cave called Pech Merle in Southern France. The caves were created some 2 million years before by underground rivers. After traveling deeper and deeper into the cave, they came upon something incredible—something that no other human had seen for nearly 25,000 years—a series of murals and engravings that covered the walls of the cavern. There were hand-drawn pictures of a wooly mammoth, spotted horses, cattle, reindeer, and silhouettes of human hands.

These prehistoric people did what we all at least *try* to do: they left their mark, and they signed it with the hand that drew the animals. These "signatures" were made by holding their hand up to the wall and then blowing charcoal or ochre over the hand. When the hand was moved, what was left was an outline. To me, the handprint shouts, "I was here!"

It may have been intended for the next group who would wander into these protective caves during the Ice Age. We'll never know. Regardless of the intention back then, what we can take from this now is that before there was even a system of writing, people had a desire to leave their mark on the world.

And now, 25,000 years later, I'm writing about it and asking you to ponder the following questions:

Have you left your mark?

Will the world remember your name or what you've done in a hundred years?

What about your family?

Now, you need to understand I'm not simply talking about being successful. I'm talking about the answer to this question:

Has the life you've lived on this earth made a difference?

I am writing this book to leave a mark. I have watched human behavior from a vantage point that most have never had the opportunity to do. Thus, I want to share these experiences, lessons, coachable moments, and epiphanies that have changed my life *and* the lives of those I have observed.

My path led me to a point where I don't have to "work" for anyone else for the rest of my life. I had friends who kept moving me down the line by asking me to speak around the country and introducing me to people who opened the opportunity to put my experiences into a book.

I believe there was a reason I was given these opportunities, and if I were only to share them with a small group of people, I believe that would be very selfish on my part. Instead, I intend to leave my mark and inspire scores of people through both my stumbling and success.

A Legacy of Leaving a Mark

I've spoken at length about what a prominent figure my mom was in my life, and now I'd like to tell you a little bit about my dad.

Pops was a big man. Six-foot-four inches tall, to be exact. He climbed the corporate ladder, not through compromise, but by doing the job at hand better than anyone else could do it. He was a take-no-shit kind of guy. When I was young, my friends would come over to my house after school. They all timed their departure upon the arrival of my father from his 14-hour days (that he worked 7 days a week). He scared them. Hell, he scared me! Now, let me be clear: I was never beaten, but the upspoken threat of "I brought you into this world; I can take you out" was always an option.

My father, Dallas Carlisle, left his mark on this country by building a grain line from the fields of the Midwest to the Great Lakes, and then he built a coal line from the coal fields in Wyoming to the Great Lakes. These lines of commerce are still used today. Had he been willing to "play the game," he might have eventually run the entire railroad. He had advanced from pounding rails to the position of assistant vice president and division manager. Though he didn't have a college education, he earned each promotion by taking the toughest jobs and making them profitable. He didn't want to sit in an office. He wanted to always be moving, driving his people as hard as he drove himself. He was a grinder. He never had time to waste doing frivolous things. He was driven to make everything around him run better. Whether it was at work or at home, he would never accept good when great was in reach.

He and my mom, Marian, also left their mark on the family. Despite neither of my parents graduating from college, all five of their children earned their college degrees. All five of us are driven individuals, each following our own paths to make the world we always dreamt of come to life. Mom and Dad didn't tell us what to be. There was always the understanding that whatever it was that we chose to do, we just needed to be the best at.

That was my upbringing. I was blessed to have two parents who were driven to maximize every opportunity, whether it was guiding their children along their paths or building a career by making all the bad jobs into great opportunities. Both of these take great effort and focus. Whether you come from a two-parent family or not, you still control the most important element in the equation: Yourself. (And how hard you are willing to work to maximize every opportunity that comes your way.) If you grew up in a rough environment, do you use that an excuse, or do you use that as a catalyst that will help make your life memorable for generations to come? The choice is yours; it has been and always will be. How far do you want to take your life?

So how does one leave his mark? Leaving your mark is about so much more than having more money, winning more games, or any outward sign of "success." Most people leave their mark without even trying—it's just the way they live their life. They don't wake up every morning wondering how they can get "likes" on their social media; their focus is about how they can make life better for all people. Making a difference doesn't take millions of dollars. Making a difference doesn't take outside attention. Making a difference is a mindset that you live with every single day of your life. It can happen in your house, on your block, or in your neighborhood. In your personal world, you can leave your mark as a great parent, a great spouse, a great son or daughter. In your work world, you don't have to run the company to make a difference. You must set a standard every day that each person strives to obtain.

Gifts: How to Leave Your Mark

Think about the people who have already left their mark on the world, whether still alive or not: Bill Gates, Bruce Lee, John Mellencamp, Mahatma Gandhi, Oprah Winfrey, and the list goes on and on. What do they all have in common? In my research and observation, I've noticed five things that set people apart to leave their mark on the world. These people are:

1) Grinders (Hard Workers)

2) Internally Driven (Highly Motivated)

3) Focused (Goal-Oriented)

4) Transformative (They Change and Effect Change)

5) Synergetic (Path Makers)

In other words, they used their G.I.F.T.S. as they moved along their chosen paths.

When one takes their skills and talents to the top of their chosen field and then applies the GIFTS that helped them along the way, they are right on track to leave their mark. But when they expand these GIFTS to not only help themselves but help others, they are well on their way to a path of significance, not just success.

So… what do I mean? Let's explore.

Grinders (Hard Workers)

First off, those who leave their mark are not lazy. Rather, they "make" things happen through their hard work. Often, this means that they don't stick to an eight-hour schedule. They are not clock-punchers. They will do whatever it takes, no matter how long it takes, to accomplish their dreams.

Grinders don't find their work mundane. They understand what may be seen as number crunching or busy work is essential to accomplishing what they set out to. Grinders take the mundane and build the foundation for their success off it.

How many mindless hours did Bill Gates type in code before he made his billions? Had he not put in the work, would he be doing what he is doing today? I really doubt it. The Beatles played hour after hour in German bars and clubs, building the foundation for what they would become. If you read any of the documentaries, books, and articles about this band, you'll see that most of them make it abundantly clear how invaluable that time was during their early years.

To become significant, we need to understand that good things never come easy. The extra effort we give daily will determine how we will reap the benefits of our hard work.

Internally Driven (Highly Motivated)

Mark makers are also self-starters. Instead of being driven by external factors, they move forward because of their internal desire to be better and leave what they have known before behind them. It may be an abusive childhood, a death in the family, or simply setting goals that pushed them to be the best. As I mentioned before, having the guts to strike off in a different direction and refuse to follow the pack doesn't come easy. Too many people don't understand this drive and will either try to slow you down or take you off your course. However, the best can never be detoured from their destiny. It matters too much to them.

Staying motivated is difficult, and many people grow weary and constantly need to be pulled along. Others need immediate satisfaction and will stop once they become successful. But those who are geared for this wake up every morning excited about the possibilities in front of them.

In the end, having the drive to keep moving forward is a continuation of what made you successful in the first place. Why coast when you have accomplished a dream? Keep pedaling and moving toward the next goal—and use your ambition and drive to help others attain *their* dreams.

The great martial artist and movie star Bruce Lee was one of these people. He didn't wait for someone to come up with a better fighting style; he developed his own. He didn't wait for people to make better movies; he made his own. His short life was a prime example of a driven individual. His writings and interviews still help people reorient themselves to get back on the road they were meant to be taking.

Focused (Goal-Oriented)

Goal-oriented people are not content to just sit around and watch things happen. They are focused on being the best. Their goals leave no variance. They were not content in their message only being heard by their constituency or their country, and their attention to detail and unwavering dedication to accomplishing what they set out to do made them who they would become.

I love the line from a fictional movie about Ludwig van Beethoven: "God whispers into the ears of some, but He shouts in mine!" These are the thoughts of a focused individual. When you watch others go through their day texting, sipping coffee, chatting on the phone, checking their Instagram or their Facebook account instead of doing their best work to accomplish the goal of being the best, you can be sure they won't be the mark maker they *could* be.

John Mellencamp believes that to live an artist's life, he needs to create something every day. It doesn't matter if it is a song, a poem, a bookshelf, or a painting, he will create something every single day. He is focused because he understands what he's made to be doing on this earth. He creates. It may be music, or it may be his work on raising funds for farmers who have struggled around this country; whatever it is, he is making life better every day because he is focused on living an artist's lifestyle.

Transformative (They Change and Effect Change)

Rarely are those who leave their mark born with all of the skills that set them apart from everyone else. These people take what they were born with and continue to expand upon their talents. In the same vein, their vehicle of success isn't necessarily where they end up making their mark. They continue to evolve as humans. As they move forward, they take their gifts and use them as a ladder to push them further and further.

Once these types of people reach the end of their first career, they see that there is still so much more to do. When they finish one dream, one that took all of their hard work and their focus, they see that they may have missed opportunities to make a difference along their way up. Once they finish accomplishing their first dream, they can then move onto their next.

Transformational people not only evolve and adapt, but they also become teachers. They not only change themselves; they also reach out to help *others* make a change. They help them get over a sticking point or refocus and find a better path.

The great statesman Mahatma Gandhi started as a lawyer but evolved to become a leading voice in changing the structure of India's leadership from a colony to that of an independent country. In the end, he became the iconic figure for peaceful protest. He not only transformed himself through his evolution as a person, but he was able to help those around him transform by understanding that each human has a value that cannot be denied by race, religion, or birth status.

Synergetic (Path Makers)

Mark makers didn't get to their position on their own. These people are gifted bridge-builders. They bring people into their circle who not only help them but are helped by association. The mark makers will continue to enlist people to their cause as they move along their path because successful people stay with what works, and that doesn't include going it alone. The benefits of this coalition will then be passed on to others.

Too many people become jealous and spiteful of others' successes. They want to always be the spring that people return to, even when they are no longer filling people with life-giving knowledge that they need in order to be successful.

These synergetic people are not jealous of others climbing farther. When we take the baton from these greats, whether it is a teacher, a historical figure, or someone who you look up to, and you move farther down the road, we validate their hard work and sacrifice. The people who have torn down walls and fought battles long before you allow *you* the chance to make your own mark.

Oprah Winfrey was able to fight through an abusive childhood. She did what she had to do to make it as an actress and, eventually, became a show business icon. Her climb was arduous, and most would have quit before they attained the top of the mountain. But because she fought the fight, she has left a roadmap for the rest of us to follow. To her credit, she didn't stop when she got to the top; she has continued to clear paths to allow others to follow in her wake so they can accomplish their own dreams. The people whom Oprah has helped now may follow her example and continue to do this themselves. The power of joining with others to make everyone better is a great gift.

Success vs. Significance

The whole process of moving from someone who simply has goals and dreams, to becoming successful, and then pushing through to reaching a point of significance and leaving your mark is nearly impossible, right? These "mutants" must all be extraordinarily smart, come from wealthy families, or hail from big cities (or maybe another planet), right? Of course not. Why would I spend the time and effort to write this book if that were true? In fact, there are stories of people maximizing their potential all around us if we look for them.

Let me show you how common the uncommon truly is. Let's take a pretty non-assuming state: Minnesota. This is a simple one. Three people who left their mark who can be claimed by the state of Minnesota. I present to you Robert Zimmerman, "Sparky" Schulz, and Alan Page. That was pretty easy. Let me continue on… wait, you don't know who these people are? And you're wondering how they made their mark? Let me show you.

Two Paths Converge

Robert Zimmerman was born in Duluth, Minnesota, but grew up in the small community of Hibbing. Hibbing is about as far off the beaten path as you can get. It's way up there.

Robert fell in love with what would be his lifelong passion very early on. He worked on his craft through high school, eventually heading south in 1959 to attend the University of Minnesota. Robert later dropped out of college because it failed to further his desire to be a performer.

After dropping out of college, Zimmerman headed to New York in 1961 to work on his passion of music and meet his idol, Woody Guthrie. As he learned from other musicians and artists, his passion only grew. His talent grew as well, proving that his move from Minnesota was the spark that would ignite his professional fire. It also brought about a name change—instead of Robert Zimmerman, he would forever be known as Bob Dylan.

Dylan made his first folk album in 1962 entitled *Bob Dylan*. Even though it only sold 5,000 copies, he wasn't deterred. He knew he was close. His second album was labeled as a "protest album." This project showed the influences of Guthrie as well as Pete Seeger and made him the voice of his generation.

In 1963, Dylan and Joan Baez sang at the March on Washington, sharing songs from his third album, *The Times They are a-Changin'*. His success was not only felt by folk music lovers, but by all cultures fighting for equality.

In 1965, Dylan took his early love for rock & roll music and his newfound love for folk music and combined them, changing the music landscape forever. This merging of his two paths took him to the top of the music world.

Rolling Stone magazine named Dylan's "Like a Rolling Stone" the best rock & roll song ever. Eventually, he would be the recipient of an Academy Award for his work on the movie *Wonder Boys*. In 2010, he was named to the Rock & Roll Hall of Fame. In 2012, he was awarded the Presidential Medal of Freedom by President Barack Obama. He earned the Nobel Prize in Literature in 2016 and has collected 11 Grammy Awards and 47 nominations. At this time, Dylan has 39 studio albums and 13 live albums to his credit, and I have no doubt that number will continue to climb.

For many, this list of accomplishments alone would make Dylan "significant." However, what truly makes him significant is not the 125 million records he sold but the voice he gave to the civil rights and anti-war movement and the scores of people he influenced in the music world. *That* is what makes him significant. Dylan's influence is still felt today in the storytelling songs of all genres. Artists such as Jimi Hendrix and the Beatles, the Rolling Stones, Kurtis Blow, Beastie Boys, Kid Cudi, Merle Haggard, and Wyclef Jean have all borrowed parts of Dylan in their songs.

Not Just a Comic Strip

"Sparky" Schulz was born in Minneapolis, Minnesota, growing up across the river in St. Paul. "Sparky" met with discouragement early on, submitting drawings to the high school yearbook only to get rejected. It would have been easy to move on to another path. But he stuck it out. After graduating from Central High School, he began to study drawing and cartooning through Federal Schools, a correspondence school, until he was drafted into the military in 1943 and served to the end of the war in 1945.

Schulz continued doing small lettering and comics in small newspapers, and even the *Saturday Evening Post*. In 1947, he started drawing a recurring comic strip entitled "Li'l Folks" for the *St. Paul Pioneer Press*. This strip evolved into *Peanuts*, which became nationally syndicated.

From 1950 until Schulz's death in February 2000, Charlie Brown was shown in comic strips around the world. In 1965, the animated special *A Charlie Brown Christmas* became a nostalgic part of holiday traditions. Because of this success, Schulz put out an animated special for each holiday, totaling 30 television specials. Apollo 10, the dress rehearsal for the landing on the moon with Apollo 11, even named the command and lunar modules Charlie Brown and Snoopy. Charles also was awarded an Academy Award, two Emmy awards, and a Congressional Medal of Honor.

Charles M. "Sparky" Schulz was responsible for 40 books and 18,250 comic strips. His passion could be seen in newspapers in 75 countries and 21 languages, with more than 355 million readers worldwide. Today, more than 20 years after his death, reruns of Charlie

Brown, Snoopy, and the gang can still be found in thousands of newspapers around the world.

Most people would see this as a pretty significant life. But all the strips and awards only brought him to the level of being *successful*. What put him in the elite status of *significant* is the effect he had on politics and world news. Using his sarcasm and sharp wit for political satire, he used the voices of his characters to speak to the readers about world issues. In my opinion, this is why his comic strips and characters are still viable today. The issues he wrote about over 50 years ago still find similar circumstances today!

Artists such as Bill Keane (*Family Circus*), Bill Watterson (*Calvin & Hobbes*), Morrie Turner (*Wee Pals*), and Garry Trudeau (*Doonesbury*) all leaned on Schulz as a major influence to show that a comic strip can do more than make you smile; it can also make you pause and consider what is happening around you.

More Than a Football Star

Alan Page was born and raised in Canton, Ohio. As a young man, he worked on construction sites, one of which would eventually become the Pro Football Hall of Fame. Little did he know at the time that he was working on the place where he would be enshrined several years later!

After finishing high school, Page was offered a scholarship to play football at Notre Dame. A great education and "Knute Rockne," whose success made Notre Dame synonymous with championship football, were the main factors of why he picked the Fighting Irish over other schools that recruited him. As a senior in 1966, he was named to the All-American Team and helped lead Notre Dame to a national championship.

He was picked in the first round of the NFL Draft by the Minnesota Vikings. Page was one of the members of a defensive line that would be nicknamed the "Purple People Eaters." This defensive line was so good that in 1969, they were *all* placed on the Pro Bowl team. Page would be named the NFL's Defensive MVP 5 times, one of the top 22 players in the NFL (All-Pro) 6 times, and in 1971, he was named the NFL MVP. As a member of the Vikings, he helped the team get to four Super Bowls. In his 15 years as a starter in the NFL, he never missed a single game, playing 236 straight.

One of Page's most overlooked accomplishments was that he had sacked opposing quarterbacks 40 times in 3 years… between 33 and 36 years old. This spoke to just how well he took care of himself. To be able to put up numbers of people 15 years younger than him was no small feat!

In 1988, Alan Page was named to the Pro Football Hall of Fame in the very building he helped to build in Canton, Ohio. In 1993, he was named to the College Football Hall of Fame. In 2018, he was awarded the Presidential Medal of Freedom by President Donald Trump.

Does having a great football career make him significant? In the area of football, I would say yes, but in the grand scope of things? No. But his story isn't over.

What I haven't told you yet was how, when he was just 8 years old, the Supreme Court case *Brown v. Board of Education*, made front page news. Page saw a glimmer of hope for how the legal system might end the oppression that people of color had lived under, and from that time on, he wanted to be a lawyer.

While playing in the NFL, Page took law classes and graduated from the University of Minnesota with his Juris Doctorate in 1978.

By 1979, he was working in a law firm, and in 1985, he was appointed Special Assistant Attorney General for the state of Minnesota. In 1992, Alan Page was elected to the post of Associate Justice of the Minnesota Supreme Court. In 1998, he was elected again, and this time he received more votes for the position than any-one in Minnesota's history. He won re-election in 2004 and 2010. Eventually, he was forced to leave office at the age of 70 because of Minnesota's mandatory retirement rules.

In my eyes, this is what made Alan Page significant. His path was always to be a lawyer. Along the way, he happened to be one of the best football players to ever play the game. In the end, he was able to continue to help all those around him with his courage and desire to make the world a better place.

Is it Repeatable?

I know, that was a bit like reading a textbook. Forgive me; it's my history teacher coming out. I just felt it was important that you got the full picture of each of these amazing men.

Did you notice that each person I just mentioned has not only become the best at their profession but also profoundly affected the people who came after them? They paved the way to make it easier for us to travel a little farther. They used their GIFTS to take them from success to significance. Dylan could have gotten his degree at the University of Minnesota, Schulz could have become a commercial artist, and Page could have played football and retired. However, because they followed their passion and decided to blaze their own trails, they have left their mark.

The question then must be asked, if they can do it, can it be done by others? Is it repeatable? Can *you* do it again and again, or did you just get lucky?

The desire to make greatness repeatable is the true test to see if someone actually left their mark. Can what you've accomplished be done again and again and again? Do you wake up every morning excited about the challenges that are in front of you? Can you be consistent with your focus and mindset?

Nowadays, too many people are one-offs. A "one-off" is a person who does something once and can't back it up. We see it in music all the time. The "one-hit wonders"—those who put a song at the top of the charts but never seem to get back to that level. We also see it in business. Someone founds and builds a company, sells it for millions, and then spends that money trying to strike gold again. And, of course, we see it in sports. I have personally watched a backup quarterback throw six touchdown passes in one game and get a big contract from another team the following season, only to be beat out by a rookie quarterback. They just got lucky, so they have no real understanding of how to repeat their success. Still, they want all the accolades of someone who put in the work.

I learned about the concept of being "repeatable" by Nolan Richardson, the great basketball coach at the University of Arkansas. Tim Weiss, the assistant strength coach at the University of Arkansas, was running the basketball off-season training program during the spring I was a graduate assistant in the weight room. Tim had picked me to help him work with the basketball team.

Tim and I had worked on a training program that combined strength work, agility work and plyometrics (jumping drills), flexibility, and conditioning. As the off-season was about to come to an end, the athletes were testing out at higher levels than they had in the past. On this particular day, we were testing their vertical jump. The vertical jump measured how high an athlete could jump without using a step into it. Simply squat down and jump as high as you can. Coach Richardson had come to watch the testing.

Athlete after athlete completed the drill flawlessly, each jumping higher than they had ever jumped before. Tim and I were really excited about the results being put up by the team. During the testing time, Tim turned to Coach Richardson and said, "These guys are going to jump out of the gym this season." Coach Richardson simply stood there, watching the athletes with his face blank and arms crossed. He was never one for small talk.

He looked at Tim and said, "Can they do that more than once?"

"Coach, we can do the test again—anytime you want to do it."

Coach Richardson chuckled and said, "Coach, I don't doubt your hard work made them better, but can they jump the same height more than once? Can they jump the same height two or three or four times in a row? If my guy jumps 35 inches on the first jump but can't jump back up right away, we won't win many games. Basketball isn't a single effort sport; you might have to jump multiple times to tip a ball in the basket or get the rebound. If they can only jump really high one time, they can't play for me. The drills need to make each action repeatable with the same consistency. Even if the player can only jump 30 inches, can he do 30 inches each time without staying on the ground?"

We hadn't thought about it that way. Instead, we were locked in the old testing standards that everyone used. One lift, one jump, one throw. From that day forward, my preparation for the season always pushed the idea I learned from Coach Richardson.

"Is it repeatable?"

To make a significant impact upon his basketball team, there was no place for one-off occurrences, whether it be a vertical jump, a tipped ball, or a great effort and hustle. This was what Nolan Richardson demanded from his team, and he sculpted them to be successful because each player understood and bought into what was being asked of them. Coach Richardson leads a life of significance not only because of his coaching but because of his work *outside* of coaching as well. He was a trailblazer for other coaches of color getting the opportunity to coach at the highest levels.

Coach Richardson stressed the repeatability of a task because it brought about *consistency*. When one is consistent, there comes a comfortability that allows a flow and balance, which equates to harmony. This harmony can be seen in successful sporting teams, businesses, and most importantly, in a focused life. Without harmony that can be repeated, an organization will fall into chaos. Chaos is defined as complete disorder and confusion.

When an organization loses its consistency, it obviously impacts their flow, balance, and culture. But those who remain consistent in their approach can still function at a high level—even amidst chaos. Successful people are able to thrive even in chaos because they have allowed their preparation and practice to build a repeatable foundation. If our work remains repeatable, whether in our personal lives, in our jobs, or by others on our team, we will always be moving forward.

My Mark

The day I stepped out of the football world for the last time, I was excited about the opportunity to continue my journey. I became a full-time strength and conditioning coach. I was able to help four teams win championships over the next 20 years. We moved three times (Knoxville, Los Angeles, Seattle), and each stop was an opportunity to grow and help others along their path. When the opportunity came to leave the coaching profession, I did it without hesitation. Within four months, I had sold my house and moved my family to Arizona. I knew I could lend a hand to my brother, who had been overseeing the care of my 90-year-old father. Professionally, all I needed was a city with an airport that could get me from one speaking engagement to the next. Personally, I was tired of being forced inside by the weather. In Arizona, I can be outside writing and working under my covered patio. The heat is abated by the use of foggers and a portable swamp cooler that keeps my writing area at 80 degrees no matter how hot it is in the sun!

I had been planning on this day for several years—the day I could look back on my path up to this point and allow the advantage of perspective to understand how it all happened. I write every day. Whether I travel or not, I am writing.

I have always written. I find it a great way to really understand what's in my head. Speaking out loud is easy, as the words evaporate into the air. However, when you write, you need to carefully formulate your ideas. As you write each letter of each word, you measure that idea. Your internal bullshit sensor knows when you are posturing or if you are speaking the truth. Even when I was coaching, I would write every day. Most of those notebooks are full of answers to the training issues I was confronted with. The other writings were about understanding myself—*my why, my what* and *my who*.

And now, what you hold in your hands is the start of a new journey and a new path, paving the way for you to leave your mark on the world—whatever that may look like.

It's Your Turn

I have just walked you through the thought process of leaving your mark on the world. We saw that mark-making had a primitive beginning, when survival was the most important thing from the time you woke up to the time you went to sleep. Since we're not fighting off saber-toothed tigers anymore, we can take this energy that was built into our genetic systems by our pre-historic brothers and sisters and work to make our lives significant from the time we wake up until we go to sleep.

We owe the previous generations that much—the admiration for being the first to leave their mark, paving the way for you to do the same. In today's world, scoreboards are shut off in youth competition because people really think everyone can be a winner. In case you don't know by now, I'm not that type of person. If competing to be the best is not "winning," then I'm pretty sure I've missed the point for my entire life. When my son's kindergarten teacher said his only issue was that he always wanted to be first, I didn't understand the problem. I feel badly for those students and parents who believe the world will wait for them to decide to get up and get in front… because it doesn't. The world will always be about deciding if you are going to lead or be led. The difference is that when you lead, you're on a trajectory to accomplish your dreams. When you sit back and wait, you will be led. You will follow someone else and accomplish *their* dreams.

It is your decision.

When we lose the desire to be successful, we can never truly live a life of significance. I say this because the way to become successful parallels the path to significance. The ability to grind through the labors of building a foundation, to be internally driven so we don't have to wait for someone else to tell us when to go to work or when we are done. The ability to focus on what is important and ignore those who try to deter us from accomplishing our goals, transforming from who we are to who we are supposed to be. And lastly, to have the power of synergy to draw others to us to complete greater tasks.

When we use our GIFTS, we can blaze a wide, clear path that generation upon generation can follow as they strive to make their own mark.

And now, that is what I give to you.

The choice is yours: Move or Die.

Keep Moving Down the Line!

> **Life is like riding a bicycle. To keep your balance, you must keep moving.**
> **—Albert Einstein**

I lost my father, Dallas, during the writing of this book. During his last days, he could not get comfortable. In fact, he fell several times trying to get out of bed or out of his recliner. He didn't know where he was going; he just knew he had to *move*. The hospice nurse called it "terminal restlessness," which was part of the dying process. The mind and body have a need to continue to move. Even as we prepare for the final sleep, our genetic impulses won't let us go silently into the great beyond.

This book is your guide as you boldly move down your life's path. The stories I have shared with you are examples of the principles that I have found necessary to maximize our God-given potential. As you begin to follow and live out these principles, you are carving out a path to lead a life of significance.

As this book comes to a close, I want to encourage you: Don't wait. Start your pursuit of ultimate success today. Don't let the steps outlined in these chapters just be words on a page—let them shape the way that you move forward. And let me remind you: it's only scary because you are doing something new.

I want you to recall all of your firsts: when you pedaled a bike for the first time, walked to school by yourself, learned how to drive, went on your first date, got your first job, and encountered your first epiphany. You survived all of these firsts by doing what? That's right. You survived by continuing to move forward. Now you must continue to take steps out of your comfort zone and move toward living the life you have always dreamt of.

Remember to be a student of life. Take time to understand who you are and where you are truly meant to be. Trust yourself and earn the trust of others through living a life of consistency. Don't be afraid to speak your dreams into existence. Weather the storms and the hardships through your effort and perseverance. Don't be afraid to take risks that don't make sense to anybody but you. Surround yourself with people who are willing to tell you the real truth; not just what you want to hear. Own your mistakes of the past by moving forward and doing better in the future. And finally, leave your mark as not just being successful, but as one who became significant by making the world a better place for all people.

This life we lead is all about movement. Either you're moving forward, or you've become stuck and you're just waiting for it all to end. It's up to you to decide which way you're going to go. You must take control.

Now, go on and MOVE!

The Game Plan

For every winner,
there's a loser.
And that person
didn't really need to
lose. They just didn't
understand
the game plan.
—Buzz Aldrin

Now that you've finished this book, you may be saying, "What's next?" I hear you! And I've got a plan for you.

For 35 years, I was part of football organizations that developed a game plan every single week. I will tell you from experience that no matter the level, whether high school or NFL, the plan wasn't developed the day before the game. In fact, most of the time, the planning started *months* before game week.

So how do you even begin formulating a game plan? Well, it starts with an understanding of who the team is. Then, you expand into assessing the strengths and weaknesses of the team. Eventually, you get into the potential of the team. Once these individual boundaries are developed, the coaching staff will dig into the inner workings of shoring up what the team doesn't do well as a whole (while continually improving the strengths). Each member of the team is forced to become better so that when the week of the game comes, each member is prepared for what is going to happen on game day.

This section has been written with this planning methodology in mind. Starting with a broad plan, and then working toward the individual skills and traits needed to carry out the plan. Each day, a new learning opportunity is being introduced. As you become adept at each step, much like an athlete does during practice, you will be ready when opportunity comes. This takes a lot of hard work, but no more than you are capable of giving.

So, without further ado, let's put together that game plan. The following is a sample of my Game Plan Workbook. Before we dive in, you'll need to get out a notebook and a pen and be prepared to write down the answers to the questions that I ask. If you're really serious, you'll want to journal your progress through each stage. Each chapter is a preparation point, and the assignments that follow will be the practice points to get you ready for your next opportunity.

Once you have finished the Game Plan, I encourage you to go through the process again in about six months. Sometimes you will find the answers to be the same. But you will also notice that other answers have changed a great deal. You may find some of the assigned tasks have already been accomplished and are in play. This is an excellent way to expand your thinking and your work to move farther down the path toward living a life of significance.

Take your time as you go through this process. Refer back to the book often, as the more you read the stories of those who have accomplished *their* goals, the easier it will be for you to see how you can get to where you have always wanted to be.

In the end, you will find out what is really important and what isn't. I went from thinking I was on this earth to win football games to eventually finding the truth to be something totally different. It wasn't about ME winning; it was about helping people get on their path and achieve their dreams. It took me several years to finally be able to see my Game Plan come to fruition, but I never lost faith in the process. Funny how things work out like that.

Now, get on with it! It's time to MOVE forward!

CHAPTER 1

HARD LESSONS

In **Chapter 1**, I talk about learning about who you really are through addressing a series of "sticking points." When I speak to groups of people, one of the first questions I ask is: "What did you want to be when you were 10-12 years old?" To me, this is the time for dreaming. No matter where you come from, you still have a pretty open road to possibilities. It's not until we get older that people start to tell us who we are and what we can't do. And, for some reason, we start to believe them.

So, I want you to do me a favor. I want you to make three lists. The first list is what you always wanted to be when you were a child. Then I want you to make a list of who you wanted to be when you were between 15 and 21. The third list is what you dream of being now. Though there are multiple spaces here for different options, you may have only had one or two. That's perfectly fine. The point of the exercise is simply to remember.

1	1	1
2	2	2
3	3	3
4	4	4
5	5	5

Assignment I: Now, go back over that list, starting with the first from when you were a child. What prevented you from becoming what you had dreamt of before the hard lessons of life came down on you? Now, look at your second list. What dissuaded you from pursuing your dreams? Are those obstacles still in your way? Finally, look at your last list. What do you need to do to obtain those dreams?

Assignment II: I want you to look at each list again. Do you see similar areas of focus continually coming up? If you aren't in that profession or position in your life, I want you to do some research on what it takes to pursue your dream and begin building a path to obtaining the position you always wanted to have.

CHAPTER 2

WHICH ONE ARE YOU?

In **Chapter 2,** the gentleman at the bar tells Doug and me about the three cowboys who all did the same work, with the same pay, but treated their positions completely differently. When you really look at the characteristics of each cowboy, I want you to ask yourself:

1. Which one are you most of the time?

2. Which one are you in the hard times?

3. What is preventing you from being the third cowboy ALL of the time?

Assignment: Go back to the book and review the story of the three cowboys. Make a list of ways you can adjust your work ethic and attitude to more closely resemble the third cowboy. When you are committed to being better in all aspects of your life, I can assure you that you will find yourself well on the way to leading a life of significance.

Chapter 3

The Deep End

In **Chapter 3,** I speak about the importance of TRUST. While trusting others is difficult, oftentimes the hardest thing for people to do is to trust *themselves*. It's challenging to trust that they are good enough, that they are worthy, and that they are prepared to go after their dreams. The first thing I want you to do is to make a short list, no more than five things, that make you unique. It might be the ability to sing, or make people laugh; the gift of hospitality or being an amazing cook, or the ability to complete any task that is asked of you. It might be as small as the ability to stand on one foot. Write these things down here:

1.

2.

3.

4.

5.

Assignment I: When you look at that list, can you identify what is missing from what you dream of being and who you really are? Is it a lack of education, a lack of experience, a lack of opportunities, or a lack of motivation on your part? Write these things down. If you find that there is a lack of opportunity, I encourage you to ask yourself if the perceived lack of opportunity is actually a lack of motivation on your part. Often, we have missed out on opportunities to better ourselves and/or look for a position, and it's up to us to change those patterns.

Assignment II: Now, I want you to find three things you need to become better at in order for you to move down your professional and personal path. Then, begin to work on making them part of a list of things that you've learned to do better. Perhaps it's going back to school in the evenings. Or, if you want to work with animals, maybe it looks like going to an animal shelter and volunteering. If you are lacking opportunities, go to a job fair and do some networking and ask the people looking for employees what skills are needed to get into that field.

Chapter 4

Speak Your Truth

In **Chapter 4,** I talk about speaking your dreams into existence and gave several examples of how people went about this process. Now, it's your turn to follow their steps.

Assignment #1: What I want you to do is to take the three things from the second assignment from Chapter 3 and write down a plan to achieve them. When you have a solid plan in place, I would like you to tell your Four Quarters about your Game Plan. Make sure they understand it and ask them to help you to stay on task.

1. **Area of Improvement**	2. **Area of Improvement**	3. **Area of Improvement**
a. First Step	a. First Step	a. First Step
b. Second Step	b. Second Step	b. Second Step
c. (Continue Adding Steps)	c. (Continue Adding Steps)	c. (Continue Adding Steps)

When you have a step-by-step game plan, you now have a plan of attack. This process will allow you to focus on short-term goals and not be overwhelmed by the "big picture."

GRIND

In **Chapter 5**, I talk about the "Get To's" and the "Got To's" of life: the things that accomplishing your dreams will bring to you, or the opportunities you get when you are moving down your path. This is what drives most people forward. However, these are also the things that can potentially slow or even stop people on their course to become successful, leading to the "stuck-stagnate-die" syndrome. To avoid getting stuck, it is important to always keep your mind on the long-term benefits of the Get To's.

Assignment #1: I want you to make two lists of five items. The first list will be entitled "Get To." These will be positive opportunities that go along with achieving your dream. The second list is entitled "Got To." These are the things that you will have to sacrifice to obtain your dreams.

GET TO	**GOT TO**
1.	1.
2.	2.
3.	3.
4.	4.
5.	5.

Assignment #2: What are you willing to give up to achieve your dreams? Go through your daily schedule and find the pockets of wasted time that you could be using in more productive ways. If the time expenditure is not necessary for the continued advance of your life, then it needs to be removed from this list. The time that you have left is what you can utilize to make yourself better to accomplish the Got To list. It may look like a huge sacrifice. But then look at your Get To list! This should make everything worthwhile. If not, you need to dream bigger to make sure your Get To's are so good you will gladly give up the things that aren't productive in your life.

Take the Risk

In **Chapter 6**, I spoke about taking calculated risks. When we know who we are, we know what we want to become, and we know what we are willing to sacrifice. So, what kind of calculated risk are you able to take to improve your position on your way to your dream? List five possible changes you can make right now that won't completely turn your life into chaos.

1.

2.

3.

4.

5.

Assignment: After you have made your list, rate the "risk factor" from 1-5 (1 being the least risky and 5 being the most) for each. To be calculated, you need to know the upside and downside of each decision. Begin with the least risky, and make a step-by-step plan to accomplish the change and not have complete upheaval in your current life. You will find that as you tackle the small risks, the riskiest begin to be more obtainable. To do all five at once can cause serious setbacks, so remember to take your time and make slow changes in the beginning.

CHAPTER 7

THE ROAD LESS TRAVELED

In **Chapter 7**, I discuss the process of thinking outside the box. What I want you to do right now is go back through and review the Five Rs (Recognize, Research, Receptive, Reach, and React). Now, look at your current work situation and identify a process that isn't working well. Next, go back through the Five R's and develop a plan to make it more efficient.

1. **Recognize:**

2. **Research:**

3. **Receptive:**

4. **Reach:**

5. **React:**

Assignment: Now that you have the steps to make your work world better, present your Five Rs to a person that can make these changes happen. Don't be deterred if they are not as receptive as you would like them to be or come up with reasons for why your plan won't work. Just continue to work on your plan and ultimately make the company better.

Chapter 8

Leave Your Mark

The last chapter of the book (and perhaps the most important) is **Chapter 8**. In this chapter, I talk about making your mark on the world and leading a life of significance, not just obtaining success. To me, becoming significant happens when you choose to use your success to help others. I would like you to go back and review the G.I.F.T.S. section of the chapter, and for each of the letters in the acronym, write down three things that you can do right now that will improve your world *and* other people around you.

Grind:	1.	2.	3.
Internally Driven:	1.	2.	3.
Focused:	1.	2.	3.
Transformative: 1.		2.	3.
Synergetic:	1.	2.	3.

Assignment: Now that you have your list of personal changes, start with the easiest one in your Grind list and begin mapping out a plan to accomplish this step. Planning is one thing but doing is what matters. Now is the time to start working on the attitude and habits that will put you on the path to significance. If (and when) you get stuck, go back and review the examples I gave in the chapter. Remember, these were just "normal" people at one time in their life.

Once you have accomplished the first idea in your Grind list, move on to the easiest on the Internally Driven list, then continue working through all five of the easiest steps to significance. Once you finish the five, go back to the top of the list and choose the next step. Each step should enrich you as much as it helps the people around you. Remember, changing people's lives and helping them further down their path is a marker of significance.

Onward

Keep in mind that this is just a short Game Plan development guide. However, the key to the success of any Game Plan is that you are truthful with yourself. First of all, you must understand who you truly are and what you bring to the game.

If you are 5' 4" and are not very athletic, you probably won't be the starting quarterback for an NFL team. But if you love the sport of football, you can make your mark in other ways, whether it's a coach, a general manager, or even an owner of a team one day.

When I was 10 years old, I told Nate Low that one day I would win a Super Bowl. I didn't have the skill or athleticism to play in the NFL, but I *did* have the tenacity to work my tail off for 25 years and earn a position on an NFL coaching staff. This not only allowed me to win but also allowed me to help the players on *their* path to win a Super Bowl.

Where there is a will, there is always a way to become what you have always dreamt of being. Find *your* way to obtain *your* goals. Follow the Game Plan, and you will exceed even your greatest dreams!

Now, it's time to MOVE… or die.

What will you choose?

About the Author

Chris Carlisle's 35 years of experience in the classroom and in the coaching profession has inspired people of all walks of life to maximize their full potential and has made him one of the nation's most sought-after motivational speakers on the circuit.

Carlisle focuses on professional and personal development, successful habits of champions in sports and business, and the work habits and leadership principles that allowed them to climb to the top rung of their profession. The underlying tone of all of Chris's teachings is that life is too valuable to not maximize one's potential. Why live to the beat of someone else's drum when you are the only one that knows and understands the music within you. No one knows better, than you, the extent of your abilities.

After graduating from Chadron State College with a Bachelor of Science in Education, Chris went on to earn a Master's Degree in History from the University of Arkansas. His professional career started as an educator and coach at the high school level, then moved up from collegiate sports to the NFL, winning championships at every level.

Chris began his public speaking career as a presenter at coaching clinics. For the next 20 years he would expand his speaking to corporations, banking institutions, real estate corporations and commencement speeches. As his reputation as a motivational speaker grew, he left the coaching profession to focus solely on helping individuals, companies and teams become efficient successful endeavors.